Chronicles of an
American
Trucker

Chronicles of an

American Trucker

"Which Way is the Road to Happiness?"

Cliff Abbott

Dedication

For those who taught me; who befriended me; who worked for and with me and those who allowed me to work for them. For those who loved me and waited patiently for me to come home, most especially my loving wife Thresa, who still fries chicken gizzards for me. For my Lord and Savior, Jesus Christ, who sustains me and still waits for me to come home.

Contents

Preface

It's amazing how many people think the typical truck driver climbs up behind the wheel, takes a leisurely drive down the highway and then parks the truck and goes home. The average motorist believes the trucker terrorizes a few people along the way, maybe out of incompetence, or maybe out of sheer meanness. There are drivers who fit that description and many others who don't.

What many fail to acknowledge is that the driver at the controls of that 18-wheeled behemoth is a human being. We're moms and dads, sisters and brothers, husbands and wives. We come from all walks of life; from high school dropouts to degreed professionals and everything in between. In a cross-section of drivers you'll find those who are highly committed to their profession and those who don't much care, just as you will in any other profession.

All of them have stories to tell. I suppose that even accountants have stories; they exist in every job. But, at a rate of 120,000 miles a year and more, a professional driver covers a lot of territory and sees much from a perch high above the highway. Comedy and tragedy, life and death; all are parts of a trucker's daily routine.

There are more stories from the vantage point of the office. Truck drivers spend many long hours away from contact with other human beings. They tend to be very independent. Their "boss" is a dispatcher they may communicate with twice a week, and that through a satellite communications message.

I've heard it said that the ideal driver is the child who didn't play well with others, now all grown up. I think there's truth to that. In another era, most would have been cowboys, drifting with the tumbleweeds while anonymously shaping a nation. Anyone who knows them has stories to share.

Some keep their stories to themselves, while others tell only their families or maybe a fellow driver over a cup of truck stop coffee. Some tell their tales to anyone who will listen on the Citizens Band radio, and a few write them down to share with everyone.

These stories are mine. Most every word of this book is true, with a few incidental "trucker embellishments." But, if you had a time machine, you could go back to when and where each recounted event actually happened and see it for yourself. Then, you could write your own book and tell it *your* way.

Chapter 1 - Sandstone

Sometimes, the best thing you can say about your day is, "it's over." Mine started in the piercing cold as I walked into the Hurricane, WV truck stop after a sleep that was much too short. I had planned a full night's rest, but mechanical problems with the trailer and loading delays had eroded my trip time. A short nap was all I time could spare for rest. I splashed a little water on my face, snagged a cup of coffee, and headed for the truck. Breakfast would have to wait. Reasoning that everything was working fine when I had parked the truck, my hasty pre-trip "inspection" was a quick kick of the tires. Then, I was on my way into the West Virginia morning.

The Turnpike was beautiful. Frozen waterfalls cascaded from the sheer rock walls where the mountains had been cut away to make room for the road. Occasional patches of ice dotted the roadway, but they were easy enough to dodge and I kept my speed down. The brakes seemed a little sluggish, but these were mountains I was driving through and the load was heavy.

The sun was well up when I left the Turnpike for I-64 towards Virginia. Signs warned of the steep grade ahead, but I'd been dealing with mountain grades all morning and I was ready. Selecting the right gear, I downshifted and settled in for a long, slow trip down the mountain. Or so I thought.

I was determined to brake as gently as possible to avoid overheating the brakes. When gravity brought my speed to 30 miles-per-hour, I gingerly depressed the brake pedal to slow to

CLIFF ABBOTT

my "target" speed of 25. I pressed a little harder at 35 mph. And even harder at 40. To my dismay, I continued to pick up speed despite my braking efforts. A quick look in the mirror said it all. Each time I touched the brake pedal, smoke poured from the tractor wheels, but not from the trailer. A pull of the hand-valve confirmed it: the trailer brakes were not working at all. The tractor brakes were overheating in a useless effort to stop both tractor and heavily-loaded trailer. With several miles of Sandstone Mountain left to descend, I knew a crash was inevitable.

I recalled a student in truck driving school asking the instructor what to do in such a situation. We all laughed when he said; "Look for a soft spot to land." But his explanation made a great deal of sense. "If you can't avoid a crash," he said, "you might at least be able to choose what you hit. Rocks are hardest, try not to hit rocks. Big trees are hard, but smaller ones will slow you as they break or bend. Flat, grassy areas are better." I was looking now, and urgently. I could see yellow signs far in the distance and I sure hoped they said "runaway truck ramp." My speed was near 80 now, and I might not be able to hold the road in the next curve, or dodge the next car. There WAS a truck ramp, one mile ahead. Could I make it another mile?

It's kind of funny, how time seems to move in slow motion in an emergency situation. Even at the speeds I was traveling, it still took some time to come down the mountain; time that seemed to crawl. I picked up the microphone and announced to the world that my brakes were gone, suggesting that any advice another driver would care to give would be welcomed. A distant driver advised that I should be sure to steer the truck into the middle of the truck ramp to avoid turning the truck over. I thanked Him. Then I prayed.

2

I have a strong faith, and I believed that whatever was about to happen was the will of God, as it should be. My own wishes were secondary. I simply asked that His will be done, and if it could be done without excessive suffering on my part, I would be grateful. I asked Him to care for my family and said I was sorry for the times I had failed Him. Then I was ready.

Well, I would have been ready if not for that unfortunate driver who moved in front of me to pass a slower recreational vehicle. The needle on the Speedometer was beyond the last number of 85; I guessed maybe 90 miles per hour. As politely as I could, I informed said driver that he was about to receive a bulldog suppository if he didn't move back to the right lane, pronto. He did so expeditiously, and his truck became an orange blur as I shot past.

I made another curve and then there was nothing between me and the opening to the escape ramp. I tugged the end of the lap belt down tight and checked my speed one last time. The needle had reached all the way at the bottom of the gauge and started to climb the other side, almost returning to the zero position. I guessed one-fifteen, and then I stood on the brake pedal with everything I had just before entering the ramp. I was attempting to lose as much speed as possible by using up whatever brakes remained. If there was any effect, I couldn't feel it as I entered the pea-gravel truck ramp. The tractor bucked to a stop; the fiberglass hood ripping off and skittering down the mountain like a sled.

The last insult was the book-on-cassette flying out of the tape player and administering a whack to the middle of my forehead. Once stopped, I sat motionless for a moment, mentally surveying my condition and the truck's. I released the seat belt and opened the door, which brushed an arc in the pea-gravel as I pushed it open. The tractor was buried so deeply that there were no steps to descend, as the surface of the gravel was even with the floor of the cab.

The force of displacing the gravel had been great enough to rip the front axle from the truck frame. When I saw the steering tires pointed outward in different directions, I remembered my firm grip on the steering wheel and realized I had been steering a truck with no front wheels for the last portion of the ride. Later, I'd find bruises on both hips from the force of the lap belt. But I was alive and the sun was shining when the Highway Department vehicle picked me up.

A kind gentleman in a pickup truck had heard my call for help on the C.B. and I had hardly stepped out of the truck when he arrived. "You all right?" he asked and I told him I thought I was. "You won't get a ticket," he said. "I'll just take you back to the office. After you clean your britches out, we'll have some paperwork to do!" Grateful, I threw my suitcase in back and hopped in the truck.

As we descended the rest of the mountain, he asked a question. "Did it enter your mind to try to ride it out?" he queried. "Of course it did," I told him, "But, I was already going over a hundred and I wasn't sure I could hold it in the road the rest of the way down." The words had hardly left my mouth when we encountered a tight curve to the left, complete with yellow 35 mph warning signs. The mountain dropped away sharply to the right with nothing but air beyond the guard rail. Neither of us spoke; we both knew I never would have made that curve. An hour later, the paperwork was done and I was checked in to a Beckley motel.

My "once a nurse, always a nurse" wife insisted I go to the hospital for treatment of the "head injury" I had suffered from the cassette tape. "No," I said. "It's just a scratch. I'm going to get something to eat, and then I'm going to bed." She tried, but I was adamant. There were no restaurants close by, but I found a hot dog and some chips at a nearby convenience store.

I returned to find the door to my room standing open and a small man of middle-eastern appearance holding up my bed to peer underneath. He dropped the mattress and jumped 3 feet in the air when I shouted "WHAT are you doing?!" "I look for YOU," was his reply. Asked why in the world I would be under my bed, he explained in heavily accented English. "Your wife call," the poor man said. "She say you hurt head and you not answer phone because you die." I assured him I was very much alive and called the Mrs. to deliver the same news.

Then I went to bed. It had been a long day.

Chapter 2 - The Scale

It wasn't easy to tell my wife I wouldn't be home that weekend, but the opportunity was too good to pass up. The foundry was running 24/7 to meet production, and needed Sunday deliveries of Michigan sand to make molds for the engine blocks they were casting. The plant workers made double-time for working Sundays, and so did we, in a way. The freight rate per ton was double the usual, and the news got better.

The I-94 Michigan scale was still under construction. The Indiana weigh station had not been open on weekends for as long as anyone could remember. The Illinois I-80 scale house was closed for repairs. That only left the Carlock scales in Illinois and, well, there are a lot of roads to Peoria. There was little chance of getting caught if we carried a few extra tons to take advantage of the high rates. I have long since changed my attitude about such things and today would encourage any driver to keep it legal. But that one night, with some careful planning and a little luck, we would earn a week's pay.

In the line to the loading chute, we talked about our big payday while we waited. Eugene was several trucks ahead, and then three of us, Mikey, Tom, and me, were grouped together a little further back. We had already opened the top hatches, so all that was left was to pull under the chute and tell the loader via the CB (Citizens Band) radio how much to load. Once loaded, we'd weigh, print off a scale ticket and pick up our paperwork.

It wasn't long before Eugene was loaded and the line moved ahead.

I was next under the chute when I saw Eugene pulling out onto the highway. Mikey asked him on the CB if he was going to wait and run with us, but Eugene just said, "No, I gotta go" and went on. "Way to be a team mate!" was Tom's parting shot. I would have commented too, but it was my turn to load and I needed to pull into position. "Twenty-eight tons," I told the loader, three more than my usual maximum cargo. "Are you sure?" came the skeptical response. I confirmed the order, and felt the rig sag as the sand began pouring into the trailer.

Soon we had all retrieved our paperwork and three overweight rigs headed into the Michigan night. We tuned our CBs to an unused channel so we didn't tie up Channel 19 with our discussion of how we might spend our windfall. For those of you who aren't truck drivers, Channel 19 is commonly used as a "community" channel where drivers share information with anyone and everyone listening. It's considered polite to take conversations that only involve a few drivers to a different channel. Had we been on 19, we might have heard someone warning us that the scale house ahead, always closed on weekends, was doing a fine business.

Our first inkling of trouble was when I rounded the curve and saw the "open" sign. My heart sank as I picked up the microphone and informed the boys behind me. As I pulled in, I wondered how much the fine would be, and if my truck would be impounded or I might even be jailed. I slowed to the posted 5 mph and approached the scale itself, knowing that the green light would change to red as I pulled onto the platform. I looked into the windows of the scale house, expecting to see a platoon of troopers ready for business. But that's not what I saw.

Through the window, I saw one trooper. Just one. And her back was to the scale readout as she wrote out an overweight ticket for the driver at the counter. Which happened to be Eugene. His eyes were huge as he watched all three of our heavy rigs cross the scale. From his position, he could read the large, red numbers that were behind the officer's back as she dealt with Eugene's citation. But, he said nothing and the light stayed green. I managed to exhale as I rolled off the other side of the scale.

We were nearly to Illinois before Mikey broke the silence. "Do you think he'll be mad?" he asked. Tom said "Tough, he could have waited for us," but I pointed out that we ALL might have been busted if he had. We wanted to feel sorry for Eugene, but we all thought it was just desserts for leaving his team mates back in Michigan. Besides, it was just too dang funny.

As we expected, he was in a bad mood when we again met up in Peoria. I guess a $1,400 fine will do that to a guy.

Chapter 3 - Rough Riding

In another chapter, I describe the first truck I ever owned, a 1988 Mack R-model. I mention in that chapter that the ride of this truck was so rough that it deserved a chapter of its own. This is that chapter.

I was still feeling groggy when I walked into the convenience store at two in the morning, but I was guessing this was my last chance for coffee for a while. And I really needed coffee. Since my R-Model Mack rode like it had square tires, falling asleep at the wheel wasn't really a concern. It's just that the first hour of my trip would be on two-lane roads through Illinois farm country, and I needed to be alert for deer. With luck, I would make my 5 A.M. delivery in Chicago and be on my way out of the city before rush hour traffic paralyzed the Interstate. If I encountered a deer, well, I guess we were both in for a bad day.

I made my way to the coffee area and bypassed the Woofa-Leaf, Gunka-Berry, and other flavoring concoctions to find my favorite: *coffee* flavored coffee, to which I added a little cream and sugar. Even half-awake, I couldn't miss the pyramid of huge, plastic coffee mugs and the "first fill free" sign. Turns out a 28 oz. mug with a free fill was a dollar; the same price as the 16 oz. foam cup. I left the store in a considerably brightened mood, with nearly a quart of fresh, hot coffee in a free mug, and even snagged a chocolate Bavarian crème pastry for breakfast.

The Bavarian crème didn't make it to the town limit. Coffee mug in hand, I settled in for a moonlight ride in the country. After a few miles, I topped a hill to behold, unbelievably, a red traffic light in the distance. It made no sense, out in the middle of nowhere, but I soon figured out that the light belonged to a bridge that was being renovated. Traffic from each direction took turns using the one available lane, and the light decided whose turn it was. According to the sign, the construction was a mile ahead, all downhill. In the moonlight I could see at least another mile of uphill on the other side of the bridge. At a little after 2 A.M., it was clear that mine was the only vehicle on the road. That's when I made a very poor decision.

Heavily loaded and starting from a dead stop at the bottom of the hill, it would have taken an hour to climb up the other side. Red or green, I wasn't about to stop to await the permission of a temporary traffic light. I kept the Mack rolling, somewhere in the general vicinity of the 55 mph speed limit as I crossed the bridge.

Unfortunately, in the darkness I could not see that the pavement had been ground away on the bridge, resulting in an abrupt drop-off of about four inches.

The ensuing result was a café-au-lait explosion as the lid flew off of my brand-new coffee mug. The flying hot liquid soaked my clothes, of course, but the more immediate problem was visibility. My glasses were covered with a milky mess. I tore them off and flung them in the general direction of the passenger seat, only to discover that the windshield was *also* covered in coffee. Stupidly, my first thought was to turn on the wipers, but since the liquid was on the *inside*, I decided to roll down the window instead. In the mirror, I could barely see the painted center line of the highway. I knew if my trailer tires were close to that line I would at least be in the correct lane until I lost enough speed to stick my head out of the window and guide the Mack to the shoulder.

It took 45 minutes and an entire roll of paper towels to clean the windshield, instrument panel and glasses, and throw on a clean shirt. My new coffee cup remained in the puddle on the floor, and I don't think I ever found the lid. Much chagrined, I carefully obeyed all traffic laws and made delivery on time. And I never saw a single deer.

In another area of this book, I discussed the "speed bumps" created by the Illinois DOT when replacing concrete sections of highway. The new concrete was seldom finished at the same level as the adjoining sections, and the result was an up and down, bumpity-bump motion of tractor and trailer as each set of wheels passed over the repaired area. In my rough-riding Mack, the effect was a spine-snapping motion that could shake fillings from the driver's teeth.

On one trip across Interstate 80, I made the mistake of filling my large mug with fresh coffee before leaving the truck stop. I should have known there was no way to drink coffee in the bucking tractor, but I was determined. I had the coffee stains on my shirt to prove it. I lifted the mug for a sip just as I crossed another "speed bump." The resulting violence launched the coffee in the mug upward, hard enough to dislodge the top from the mug and scatter the hot liquid everywhere. The event was observed by the driver of a passing truck, who found the episode amusing. "Got a drinking problem, Driver?" he asked on the C.B. radio.

I wasn't in the mood to answer.

Chapter 4 - Fishin'

Maybe you're wondering what fishing has to do with trucking, but please bear with me. After all, it's *my* book. Every once in a while, I'd get out of the truck for some family time that often included fishing. But, this time, the story is a trucking story that involves fishing; or a fishing story that involves a truck, or something. I have other fishing stories, maybe for another chapter.

I was pulling an empty flatbed (I did a *lot* of that…) to my pickup point; a sawmill in Northern Florida. Unfortunately, it was late afternoon and I wouldn't get there before they closed. All I had to do was find a place to park for the night, and get there first thing in the morning to load.

My travels took me over a bridge; a bridge across the Suwannee River. *That* Suwannee River; as in, "Way down upon;" the song I had sung in my school days. Even better, there appeared to be a dirt road just after the bridge that led into the woods beside the river. The wheels began turning in my mind.

After few miles, I came upon a small gas station / convenience store advertising bait for sale. The guy at the counter told me that the road I had seen along the river was an old logging road that led to a large clearing in the woods. It would, he said, be more than suitable for parking a truck. I bought some basic necessities; worms, hooks, bobbers, and a nifty collapsible fishing outfit in a case that I could store in the tractor for future use; maybe $40 worth of stuff. Add a bag of fried chicken, some chips and drinks, and I was ready for a peaceful night, fishing on the banks of the famous Suwannee.

Sure enough, the dirt road was solid and there was an area large enough to turn around, which I did first so that my rig didn't get blocked in if someone else showed up to fish. It didn't take long to get settled in and baited up. Soon I was munching chicken, watching my bobber float along in the current of the Suwannee River.

Unfortunately, floating was all that the bobber did as the minutes slowly passed. I tried new bait. I tried every spot I could throw to, walking up and down the bank to find un-fished territory. Then the sky began to cloud up, and it started to rain lightly. It was starting to get dark. I determined that I was not leaving until I could say that I had caught a fish in the famous Suwannee River. Getting colder, I watched the bobber float some more. It got darker, and the rain was coming down harder.

I heard a loud splash in the distance and wondered if alligators came this far north. Or, maybe it was wild hogs; my native Floridian wife had told me that they roam the piney woods along the rivers. I was ready to crawl into my safe, warm bunk and sleep, but I still didn't have a fish. I could still see, a little, in the diminishing daylight. Just a few more minutes, I promised myself.

And then I saw it. Not really a "bite;" just the slightest wiggle from the floating bobber. "Maybe a raindrop landed on it," I thought, but there it was again. Every muscle steeled for the upcoming battle, I picked up the rod and prepared to set the hook at the next movement of the bobber. Finally, there is was;

the lurking behemoth yanked almost half of the bobber under the water's surface. I jerked the rod tip upwards and felt the hook strike home.

Actually, I didn't really feel much of anything and the force of setting the hook brought bobber, bait, and some poor juvenile bream all the way up on the bank beside me. You northerners would have called it a "Blue Gill," but in the South, that's a "Bream;" pronounced "brim." It would have taken five of them to equal the weight of the chicken wing I had consumed earlier, but that's not the point here. I had come to catch fish, and catch I did.

I gingerly picked up the little rascal and removed the hook as gently as I could, releasing him into the dark waters of the Suwannee to thrill another angler on some future day. Then I disassembled the fishing outfit, put it in its case, and threw the rest of the worms in the Suwannee to help feed my little friend and any relatives of his that might swim by.

Later, snug in the sleeper berth, I happily noted that I had, indeed, caught a fish from the Suwannee River. If I had bothered to calculate the cost of rod, tackle and bait, it probably worked out to $1,200 per pound for the fish I had caught.

Some things are worth it.

Chapter 5 - Drug Testing

Everyone who makes a living with a Commercial Drivers License knows that drug screening is a part of the job. Most have heard stories about the "old days" of trucking when amphetamines were plentiful and drivers sometimes went for days without sleep. Today, however, drugs are usually taken for more "recreational" purposes, and companies are required by law to test for them.

As a driver, I have supplied my share of urine "specimens" for the purpose of drug screening. I never had a reason to worry about the results and I never had a problem with the test. When I became a recruiting manager, one of my duties was to make sure each applicant passed a drug screen before letting them get behind the wheel of a truck.

About three per-cent of new drivers fail the drug screen. Think about that for a minute. Does it boggle the mind that a person can show up at orientation class, with the *full knowledge* that he will be tested for drugs, and end up failing the test?

A simple Internet search reveals a part of the answer. There are all kinds of concoctions that, allegedly, "cleanse" the body of those pesky illegal substances. Just mix and drink. There are recipes for cranberry-juice and vinegar cocktails that are supposed to do the same. If you don't think "cleansing" will help, there are artificial urine products available that the driver is supposed to deposit in the specimen cup instead of the real thing.

There is even one rather innovative product that comes with an, ahem, artificial "delivery device" for those drug screens that must be observed. No kidding, it is equipped with a strap-on harness and a little rubber bulb that you squeeze to start the artificial pee flowing. It even comes in several different colors to match skin tones of those from every ethnic background. As for size, I suppose the buyer could always upgrade. If you're gonna go, you might as well go *big*.

I read a funny story about a Texas prison parolee who underwent random, observed specimen collections as a condition of his release from prison. Just so you know, "observed" doesn't always mean *observed*; it means someone is in the room to make sure you are following the specimen collection rules to the letter. If there is any reason to believe that you might try to use some of the artificial product mentioned earlier, or drop a chemical into your specimen to impact the results, or even substitute your girlfriend's urine, you may be required to submit to an observed test.

At any rate, the parole officer was perplexed when the aforementioned parolee stepped up to do his business and a very audible "clunk" sound emanated from the urinal where he stood. Reasoning that no part of the human body; and especially *that* part, should make a "clunk" sound when coming in contact with the urinal, the astute parole officer searched the unfortunate soon-to-be ex-parolee.

Sure enough, he was packin'. The officer confiscated the artificial penis and artificial urine sample, and the parolee gained a great story to share with his cell mate while he finished his sentence back in the penitentiary.

My first experience in drug screening from a management standpoint involved a gentleman we'll call "Clarence." I managed a small terminal at the time for a company that had just been bought out by another. The former owners had not followed a drug screening program. The new owners did, and gave each terminal manager two weeks to get their entire staff tested.

Thursday night, at the end of his evening shift, I told Clarence he was to report to the clinic on Friday morning for drug screening. He complained that he had some super-important family event on Friday that would be ruined by taking the time to go to the clinic. I bought his story, and gave him permission to wait until the following Monday. Then, I launched myself into the pile of literature I had been sent on the subject of drug screening.

Monday came and Clarence went to the clinic to leave his little sample before reporting for his evening shift. By Thursday morning, I had received the call from corporate headquarters; Clarence had to go. The specimen that Clarence had donated had turned up positive for cocaine.

While I waited for him to show up for work, I rechecked something I had read in all that drug-screening literature. And, I found it. Cocaine, the pamphlet said, is generally out of the human system within 48 hours of being used. It might take 72 hours in cases of very heavy usage. After that, it no longer showed up in the test. I would assume that the tests used today are much better, but back then, it was 72 hours, tops.

I had informed Clarence of the testing on Thursday, meaning that 72 hours had passed by Sunday afternoon. The only way he could have come up positive on Monday is if he had used cocaine over the weekend, *knowing* he would be tested on Monday morning.

"You're firing me for failing a drug test?" Clarence asked. "That's true," I told him, "but, mostly, I'm firing you for being a *dumb ass!*"

As a recruiting manager, I usually had drug screen results back within 24 hours or so. If results were back for the whole class except for one, it was a pretty good indication that there was a problem. What many drivers don't know is that the initial testing is pretty broad; sort of an "is there anything to be concerned about?" approach. If the test shows nothing, it is reported as negative. If something shows up, additional testing is done to identify exactly what the substance is. That can take extra days. Sometimes, the substance turns out to be something that's perfectly legal and the result of "negative" is delivered.

When a controlled substance *is* identified, a Medical Review Officer (MRO) must review the results and discuss them with the driver in case there's a legitimate reason for the positive result. For example, the codeine in the cough syrup prescribed by your doctor is from the same drug family as morphine and heroin and will likely trigger a positive result for "morphine derivatives." The MRO has a chat with your doctor and, if the prescription is legitimate, reports your specimen as negative. The company never knows any of this. However, they don't give prescriptions for crack cocaine and marijuana (well, except in California and those aren't accepted by the FMCSA.)

It was sometimes amusing to watch the behavior of the driver whose test results didn't come back. Nearly all of them would first claim they were mystified. "My sample?" they'd say. "I don't *do* drugs!" As the hours passed, they'd get more fidgety. Some would get angry, and the madder they got, the more convinced I was that their test was going to come back positive, even though I could say nothing. Some threatened to sue. Sometimes, they would just announce that they were tired of waiting and leave, or simply wouldn't show up the next morning. Uh-huh.

When the results came back positive, the excuses would start. There were a few that I genuinely felt sorry for. "I twisted my ankle and my mother gave me one of her pain pills" is a fairly common scenario. Unfortunately, the pain pills contained a controlled substance, and the prescription was for mom, not the driver. It's hard to get a job with that on your record, and I felt pity, but I still couldn't make the hire.

I tried not to be judgmental when a positive test came back, but, I've heard some pretty good stories. Here are some:

- "My brother smoked a joint in the car on the way up here. I asked him not to, but I didn't have another ride." Really? You're claiming you failed a drug screen because of second-hand marijuana smoke? Actually, I've heard a few variations of this one.

- "I saw the doctor while I was in California and he prescribed marijuana for my ingrown toenail." But, the Federal government still says that if you drive a truck, you can't smoke weed, even if you have a prescription *or* an ingrown toenail.

- "I spent the weekend with my girlfriend, and I found out she uses drugs." Sexually-Transmitted-Amphetamines! Hey, that's kind of kinky!

- "I went to a party and somebody must have put something in the brownies." Yes, and I'll bet they spiked the punch bowl, too. (Actually, I know of a husband-wife team that swears this is what actually happened when they both came up positive on a random test. I still believe them. A positive drug test is a career-killer, and I still feel bad for them.)

- "I just went to the dentist for an impacted tooth and I've been taking antibiotics." Crack is an antibiotic?

- "We went to a restaurant to celebrate my new job. I *thought* that broccoli tasted funny." Good thing you didn't try the fettuccini!

- Or this variation, "My wife is Italian and a great cook. She uses a lot of spices in her cooking!" If that's true, "Honey, bring me the oregano and some rolling papers."

- "They must have mixed up the samples." Well, I guess that's possible. That's why they split your specimen into two samples *right in front of you*, and seal up the bottles *right in front of you*, and ask you to initial the seals that they put on the bottles *right in front of you*. Did you ask them to test the 2nd sample to confirm the result? After all, it's your career, right? Didn't think so.

Most of the drug screening I was involved in was for pre-employment purposes. Once, however, I was approached by a dispatcher who asked me to take a look at some messages a driver had sent over the satellite communications unit in his truck.

ZELDA IS FOLLOWING ME AND SHE HAS THE RAY GUN, said one.

I LIKE EARTH, AND I'M NOT GOING BACK, said another.

That one was followed with; I ALMOST LOST HER, BUT THEY TRACKED ME FROM THE STARSHIP AND TOLD HER WHERE I WAS.

Message after message was sent in the same vein, most mentioning something about how much he liked being here on Earth and most definitely did *not* like the ray gun that Zelda was carrying.

"What do you think he's trying to tell me?" the dispatcher asked. "I'm no expert," I said, "but I'm thinking he's trying to tell you that he really, *really* wants a reasonable suspicion drug screen." As luck would have it, we were able to alert the authorities of his impending arrival at a weigh station just a couple of miles up the road. We sent a message to the driver explaining that the police escort was just in case Zelda showed up with the ray gun. You can't be too careful when ray guns are involved, you know.

The driver tested positive for *three* different drugs and was terminated from his driving position. He was taken off in handcuffs, but I never learned what he was charged with. So, I never found out if the terms of his parole allow him to leave the

Earth, or if Zelda is still out there with the ray gun. Please, be careful.

Finally, there's the "refusal to test" category that rears its head from time to time. Few drivers are aware of the law as it regards random drug or alcohol testing, but the gist is this: if you are told to get tested; GO. The Federal regulations are pretty specific, as you'll know if you read the copy your company gave you when you were hired. You *have* read the regulations, right?

Usually, the story goes like this: the driver completes the employment application and in the space that asks, "Have you ever failed a drug screen or refused to test," he marks "No." He's surprised to learn that a refusal to test has been placed on his record. When asked for details, he says he was planning to quit that job. When they told him to go get tested, he figured he was quitting anyway, so he left. Bad mistake. The incident goes on his record as a refusal to test and gets reported to any other company he applies to. The law says it must be reported for two years, but it doesn't say it can't be reported after the two years are up. Many companies will report it much longer. According to the regulations (the ones you didn't read), a refusal is treated the same as a positive test.

I had a friend whose dispatcher told him to see a person in the safety department for an alcohol test, which involves a quick and simple mouth swab. He waited around for about a half-hour and then he found out the person who did the testing was out to lunch. He hadn't seen his family in two weeks and wasn't happy about waiting around. Finally, his impatience got the best of him and he went home to his family. He was fired and had a hard time finding another job.

My all-time favorite drug test refusal was "Merle," the new driver in orientation. He disappeared from the clinic we had taken the class to for physicals and drug tests. The guy who shuttled them to the clinic in the company van searched high and low, but Merle was nowhere to be found. Finally, they left without him.

He showed up at orientation class several hours later with a dozen red roses and a love note inside a card with little silk hearts all over it. He explained that he was so enamored of the female instructor that he just couldn't get her off of his mind. To prove his affection (and increase the chance that she would accept his proposal), he had left the clinic to visit the florist down the street and buy her card and flowers.

Merle got jilted and fired in the same day, poor guy.

Chapter 6 - Strawberry-Boy

Iwasn't very happy about the soft cast on my left foot, but I supposed I deserved it after jumping off the flatbed like that. Still, that load of steel racking on my trailer had to be delivered in southern Illinois on Monday, cast or not. I could drive, since I only used the left foot for the clutch, and I didn't use the clutch very often, anyway. But climbing in and out of a cabover tractor with crutches would be a problem, so I asked my 9-year old son to travel along to assist.

He often rode with me and we shared a fun father-son tradition when he did. He would start the trip with the nickname "Passenger-boy," and the name would change whenever something occurred that I wanted to tease him about – which usually involved food. He might become "Burger-boy" after lunch, morphing into "Chocolate-boy" after snack time, and once was "Peanut-boy" after putting a huge dent in a 5-pound bag we bought in Virginia. I loved the camaraderie we shared on these trips, and I seriously needed his help to keep my crutches close whenever we stopped.

"Crutch-boy" and I made our delivery and were dispatched on a load back to Georgia to make my doctor's appointment. We arrived early for the pickup and stopped for a leisurely fast-food lunch. After our burger and fries, we bought strawberries for dessert from the local farmer selling them in the parking lot. "Should we get the small, or large?" I asked Crutch-boy. "I want a large, too," he said. "Too?" I pointed out that the large size was a full quart of berries, but he insisted he could eat them all and some of mine, too. "Two large," I said, and we started eating them as we drove to the pickup site.

Our load was used railroad ties, which were piled along the tracks as the repair crew replaced them with new ones. We travelled a dirt road along the tracks for several miles through a pine forest to the loading area. As we waited for the crew to return from lunch, we – mostly Crutch-boy – finished the strawberries.

It wasn't long before Crutch-boy began fidgeting. At my prompting, he finally disclosed that he seriously needed to use the restroom. "We're surrounded by trees," I told him. "Take your pick." He determined to wait for more modern facilities, despite my argument that men, and especially manly men like us, had no problem urinating in the woods.

His nervous dance became more urgent, and he finally disclosed that he couldn't use the woods because he needed to sit down for this particular problem. Apparently, the massive number of strawberries he had consumed were having an unintended and urgent effect on his digestive system. "Son," I told him, "it's five miles back to town, on a dirt road, and the loading crew will be here any minute. We can't leave now. You'll have to use the woods or wait until we're loaded."

He was quiet, but only for a moment. He fidgeted some more and then repeated that he "needed to sit" and I came up with a quick solution. "Get the bucket" I told him, referring to the 5-gallon bucket we used for a trash can in the truck. "Put a clean trash bag in it, carry it out to the woods, and use it like a portable toilet. Don't forget some tissue. And when you come back, I don't want to see the bag with your business – leave it in the woods. I want my nice, *clean*, bucket back where you found it."

He didn't like it, but the strawberries gave him no choice. A few more minutes of fidgeting, and could wait no longer. He climbed into the cab and reappeared, bucket in hand, headed for the woods. "Remember," I called after him, "bring back my clean bucket, *and nothing else!*"

It seemed like too much time had passed. I was about to go search for him when he finally appeared from the woods, empty-handed and obviously distraught. I waited a couple of moments before asking, "Where's the bucket?" He silently stared at his feet. "Son?" More silence. Finally I said, "It's only a bucket, son. It's not the end of the world if we don't get it back. Why don't you just tell me what happened?"

It took a while, but with welling tears and quivering chin, he finally told me about the disaster that had occurred in the woods. With all the courage he could muster, the tears finally won as he blurted, *"The bag had a hole in it!"*

We left without the bucket. A few hours down the road, Strawberry-boy and I were finally able to laugh about it.

Chapter 7 - Texas Trouble

I hate starting a trip mad, but mad I was when my Freightliner topped out at 62 mph. The new ECM, the "brains" of the modern diesel engine, had cost me over $1,200. With a load to Texas out of the gate, I stood to earn a few badly-needed bucks to replenish my skinny billfold. But the slower speed was gonna cost me time that I didn't have much of to spare. I already had a late start waiting for my truck to be repaired and I had planned to make up some of the time with my right foot; but that wasn't happening with a 62 mph maximum speed.

I let them know about it, too, calling the repair shop from the first rest area I came to. "Not a problem," the service manager said. "They come from the factory that way. Just swing on by and we'll reset it to your specifications." "Great" I muttered. "Just as soon as I get back from Texas. If I ever *get* back from Texas."

I had plenty to stew about on my way west, and I'm still not sure how I made my delivery appointment on time. After a shower and a hot breakfast, I was in a better mood as I headed to Ft. Hood to pick up my return load. After hours of the typical government runaround, the piece of equipment was loaded on the flatbed and secured. Out the gate I went, but I didn't go far when, in the mirror, I watched the door of the loader I was hauling swing open and spray shattered glass as it slammed backwards. Apparently, the door latch had not held and the wind stream had pushed it open. Pulling to the shoulder, I knew that the freight claim for the broken window would negate any profit I made on this load. After securing the door with another strap, I headed east through Killeen.

I saw the trooper on the freeway entrance ramp, but a glance at my speedometer reassured me that I had nothing to worry about. The split speed limit was 55 for trucks and 65 for cars. I might have been at 58 or so, and the best I could do was 62 anyway, so I knew the trooper wouldn't be interested in an almost law-abiding citizen like me. But he was. The blue lights in the mirror confirmed it, and I pulled off onto the shoulder and shut the engine down, wondering why I had been selected.

I watched the officer in the mirror as he got out of his car, and it wasn't promising. He was a big guy, with a Buford T. Justice swagger, complete with mirrored sunglass lenses under his Smokey Bear hat. He strutted as far as the front of his squad car and then impatiently motioned for me to come to him. I debated bringing my paperwork and log book with, but decided that making nice would probably be my best course of action.

"Good morning," I said as I approached. "License and registration," he grunted in reply. Without another word, he disappeared into his cruiser. I assumed he was running my license through the computer in the trooper-mobile. While I waited patiently, I looked over as much of the trailer as I could see from where I stood, trying to find an obvious reason for the traffic stop.

When he stepped out of the cruiser, I could see he carried more paper than the license and registration I had given him. I braced for the worst. He handed my documents back and then barked "sign here" as he shoved a clipboard at me. He pointed to the signature block on the bottom of the citation he had written. I glanced into his mirror-shaded eyes and asked him to explain what I was ticketed for. "I clocked you at 72 miles per hour," he said, "and I'm issuing you a citation for speeding."

I tried to explain that my truck wasn't capable of doing 72 mph, and suggested that he may have clocked a passing car, since the speed limit was higher for the four-wheelers. But the more I talked, the taller he stood and the more his chest stuck out. "Besides," I said, "you just ran my license. It's squeaky clean, isn't it? No answer from Trooper Justice. "Even if I was speeding, which I wasn't, there's no warning or room for discussion? You just write it?"

The trooper leaned forward so I would get the full effect of the education he was about to administer. Jabbing his finger at my chest, he growled, "When you speed in Texas, *boy*, you get a ticket. If you have a problem with that, I can take you downtown and you can tell it to the judge."

Boy? I was already unhappy and referring to me as "boy" did not help my disposition. Still, it was evident I wasn't going to talk my way out of the ticket. I determined the better part of valor was to avoid escalating the issue, so I signed the citation and silently handed it back. But Trooper Justice wasn't done. "I thought you'd see it my way" he smiled as he handed my copy to me. "Now, let me see that log book."

I'd had enough. For just a moment I was quiet as I mentally tried to talk myself out of what I was about to do. Impatient, the trooper spoke again. "I *said*; let me see that log book." And I lost it. I pulled myself up to the full height of my five-foot, six inch frame and glared into his mirrored eyes. "Hell no," I told him. He was flabbergasted. "Are you refusing to allow me to inspect your log book?" he asked. "You catch on quick down here in Texas," I told him, shaking in my boots. "Before I cuff you and take you in," he asked, "would you like to tell me why?" And I did.

"You haven't listened to a word I've said," I told him. "So it's like this. You just wrote a bullshit ticket because you know it will cost more for me to come back here to fight it than to just pay it. I don't like it, but I don't have much choice. Now, you want to see my log book so you can write *two* bullshit tickets?"

It was obvious he wasn't accustomed to resistance, and he didn't know what to do. "Tell you what," I told him. "I do my job a hell of a lot better than you do yours. You have the authority to arrest me and then check my log book anyway. So I'll let you see my logbook with this understanding. You write another ticket, and I'll come back to Texas for the court date, and I'll beat your ass on *both* of them!"

The look on his face was priceless, but I was much too scared to enjoy it. He seemed to think it over for a moment and then he stepped back from the logbook I offered. "You'd better get on out of here," he said gruffly. "I thought you might see it that way," I offered. "By the way" I added, "it's been a lot of years since I've been a 'boy,' and I don't appreciate being addressed by that term."

He was still sitting in his cruiser, blue lights flashing, when I went over the next hill and lost sight of him in the mirror. Still, I kept a close eye on the mirrors for a long way, knowing that a line of trooper would soon appear to chase me down. I finally breathed a large sigh of relief when I crossed the border into Louisiana.

Back at the repair shop, they reprogrammed the ECM to my specified speed. I sat in the waiting room, marveling at how I had received my first and only speeding ticket during a time when my truck couldn't speed!

And, I hoped a certain trooper was having a bad day back in Texas.

Chapter 8 - Billy and the Garbage Route

Not all of my trucking experience was of the over-the-road variety. For about 6 years, I drove a garbage truck on routes in the Chicago suburbs. It was a union job; good pay, benefits, and, of course, those monthly dues. It was tough work. Unlike our city brethren, there weren't three helpers hanging off the back of the truck to load the trash. Mostly, I worked alone, loading the garbage and then moving the truck to the next stop. I once calculated that a day's work on a summer route was equivalent to climbing and descending something like 26 flights of stairs, walking 10 miles, and lifting and throwing 25 *tons* of weight, each and every day. Needless to say, I was in much better physical shape in those days. But, I digress...

Every workplace has a "character" or two, and the one that stands out in my memory was goofy William "Billy" Dubowski. Billy was a hard worker, but had the type of judgment that made you scratch your head – and wonder how it was he hadn't been fired yet. He was a resourceful dude, recycling things he found in the garbage, in the days before being "environmentally conscious" was in vogue. A drive by his home would reveal a yard decorated with "gazing globes." You've seen them, the mirrored spheres that sit atop a concrete pedestal, reflecting the world around them to the pensive "gazer(?)" Except, Billy didn't use real gazing globes. Someone would discard a busted bird bath, and Billy would take home the still-intact base. Then he'd find a bowling ball someone had thrown out; spray paint it a suitable color, and perch it atop the bird bath pedestal. Voila, instant three-holed gazing globe. At least 20 of these festooned his front yard, in every conceivable color, with the familiar three-hole grip marring the beautiful painted surface...

His dress reflected his profession, too, as he dressed himself for work from the discarded wardrobe he found. His footwear often didn't match. No, I don't mean his shoes were different colors; I mean he'd have a tennis shoe on one foot and a high-top work boot on the other. Then, there was his rain gear, which was necessary since we worked, rain or shine. The top portion was a simple garbage bag with holes cut or ripped for head and arms. The bottoms, well, they were a classic. A popular weight-loss product of the day was a pair of vinyl shorts with an attachment for a vacuum cleaner hose. The theory was, by sucking out all the air, the vinyl would cling tightly to the wearer, causing that area of the body to heat up and sweat away the pounds during moderate exercise. It isn't surprising we found a lot of them in the garbage we picked up. I can still picture Billy in his plastic shorts, two feet of white vacuum hose swinging from his hip, wearing his color-coordinated garbage-bag top and mismatched footwear.

Our routes began early in the morning, while many people were still preparing for work. It wasn't uncommon to hear Billy's voice on the company radio, announcing that an unsuspecting female resident had failed to close the curtains while getting dressed for work, giving Billy full peeping privileges that he felt honor-bound to share with the rest of us. In those days, every radio was connected, so everyone heard any transmissions on the system. In fact, the company radio was the source of much information about Billy, as we learned about many of his exploits from the chewing out he got over the radio after an angry customer called in.

There was the time Billy was suffering from, let's say, a digestive problem. Working a "carry-out" route in a ritzy neighborhood, Billy's job was to take his 60-gallon "carry-barrel" up to the home and get the garbage, saving the homeowner the task of bringing it to the curb. Billy didn't heed the call of nature when his intestines began rumbling. He continued to work, while keeping a watchful eye for the nearest bathroom. Unfortunately for Billy, high-tone neighborhoods aren't known for outdoor toilets.

Before long, Billy's situation became desperate and he could no-longer wait. Conveniently, the garbage cans in the next home were located inside the dimly-lit garage. Billy emptied the trash into his carry barrel, and in the midst of yet another intestinal cramp was consumed by a flash of brilliance; He'd use the resident's now-empty garbage can as a portable toilet! A quick look around confirmed the garage was indeed empty, and soon Billy was too, after dropping his pants and perching atop the garbage can.

His relief was short-lived, however, as the surprised lady of the house picked that particular moment to bring the kitchen garbage out to the garage. We howled, listening to Billy explaining that one over the radio, and hearing the boss' instructions to clean out the garbage can and the whole-damn-garage and apologize to the apoplectic homeowner, after finishing up with the police, of course.

As you may have surmised, Billy was well acquainted with the police. There was the time he found a pack of large "Bottle

Rockets" in the garbage. If you've used these fireworks, you know that they are a small rocket that is attached to a stick, which is typically propped up in a standing bottle to aim the device. When lit, they shoot up like a rocket, sometimes whistling all the way up, ending their short lives with a fiery bang. Billy soon figured out that he could balance the bottle rockets on the mirror brackets of his truck. Reaching out the window with a lit cigarette, he could fire off the missiles in a forward direction, giving a "Star Wars" quality to his otherwise drab garbage truck. Delighted, he targeted several fellow motorists, who weren't as amused as Billy was. Neither were the police.

Then, of course, was the BB gun incident. No, Billy didn't shoot anyone, or at least, he wasn't *caught* shooting at anyone. But, if you've ever seen some of those old BB guns, you know that the large, shotgun-like barrel they have is a fake. The *real* barrel fits inside the fake one, and is about the width of a drinking straw. The rest of the "barrel" is storage space for loading a large supply of BBs. If you remove the end of the barrel, you end the gun's ability to shoot anything, but the resulting open end looks remarkably like the business end of a nasty shotgun, a fact not wasted on Billy when he found one in someone's garbage.

You see, there was this one particular customer that was *always* late bringing his garbage to the curb. Every one of us had had the experience of backing up a half-block to retrieve this guy's garbage that wasn't there when we went by the first time. Billy was approaching that house now, and noticed that there was, once again, no garbage at the curb. His diabolical plot was set in motion.

After prepping the BB gun, he hid it in the hopper of the truck with a strategically placed bag of garbage. He blew past the offender's home, stopping at the pile of garbage at the next house. Sure enough, our ever-late resident burst from the front door, garbage bags in hand, running for the garbage truck. Billy pretended to be occupied with the garbage he had already placed in the hopper, not noticing the scurrying customer. Just as the out-of-breath customer arrived at the back of the truck, Billy spun around, pseudo-shotgun in hand. "That's far enough," he snarled, covering the offending homeowner with the gun. "Drop it right there!"

Miraculously, Billy was able to convince the police that it had all been a bad joke and the BB gun was, in fact, harmless. Billy got another chewing out, and the homeowner got a year of free garbage service, for which he was always late.

We finally lost Billy when the trash-compactor unit on his garbage truck squeezed the contents out of a gallon jug of oil someone had drained from their car. It was against the law, but homeowners often used a plastic milk jug to dispose of waste oil, hiding it inside a garbage bag so we couldn't identify and refuse to take it. In this case, the bottle had burst when compacted and poor Billy was drenched with used motor oil. Furious, he stormed up the sidewalk and stairs to the front stoop, where he laid into the doorbell like he was trying to squash a bug that wouldn't die.

The lady who answered the door was rather taken aback, as she was unaware that her husband had changed the oil in the car and certainly didn't concern herself with his method of disposal. Still dripping dirty oil all over the lady's porch, Billy continued his curse-filled tirade. Alarmed, the woman closed the storm door, keeping a barrier between herself and the oily, crazed garbage man on the stoop. Billy finally finished his lecture and stormed off, but not before shaking some of the oil running off his hands and arms onto the glass of the woman's storm door, just to emphasize his point. This time, we didn't have the pleasure of hearing Billy get chewed out on the radio. Unwittingly, Billy had chosen the mayor's house for his meltdown, and the mayor's wife had called the police. Her husband had merely called the owner of our company.

Somebody else drove his truck back to the garage that day, and I haven't heard from Billy since. He's probably lurking beneath some window, somewhere, in his plastic pants, garbage-bag top and mismatched shoes, hoping to catch a glimpse of some young lady preparing for work…

Chapter 9 - Holidays

I love holidays. One of the worst things about a career in trucking is the way holidays are different. If you get home at all, it's for a much too short period of time. The rest of the world is carving pumpkins or putting up a tree, celebrating. If you're a professional driver, the only decorations you see are either in the truck stops or hung from the light poles in the cities you pass through. Many of us on the road find the holiday spirit elusive.

Around October 1st, I'd buy a couple of those orange leaf bags they sell every autumn. They are printed with the face of a large jack-o-lantern; when filled with leaves they resemble a giant, carved pumpkin out on the lawn. I loved to cut out that
Jack-o-lantern face and duct-tape it to the end of the tanker I pulled down the highway. The duct-tape was about the same color as the aluminum tank and was barely noticeable. One in front and another in back; the pumpkins were a colorful sight that motorists could see from quite a distance. I couldn't believe how many people would blow their horns, smile and wave when they passed by; especially the kids. I really did it for the kids. The pumpkins became a tradition; other drivers would start asking when I was going to put them on when fall approached.

Christmas was even more fun. It started with the "How's my Driving" sign on the back of the trailer. Mine had a picture of Santa and said, "If this driver is naughty, call 1-800-TEL-NICK." But I didn't stop there.

Mack Truck™ is proud of their bulldog logo, and every driver of one has felt pride in the little chrome bulldog that sits on the hood and functions as a grab-handle. I was no exception, but I wanted something more for the Christmas holiday. I found a brass reindeer on the clearance rack at a department store, and an idea came to life. After sawing off the antlers, I firmly attached them to the extra bulldog I had purchased. Then, I drilled a small hole in the nose, and installed a red "bullet light," usually used to attach license plates. The result was a perfect bulldog "Rudolph," complete with light-up red nose. To complete the effect, I mounted a clear plastic bug shield, to which I attached Christmas themed decals. It was priceless, but I had one more decoration in mind.

On the clearance rack at the department store where I purchased Rudolph's antlers were these light-up Santa faces, complete with a big Santa smile, rosy cheeks and a red hat. I bought two, and replaced the lights inside with 12-volt lights that could be powered from the tractor's electrical system. I attached one to each end of the tanker, and wired them in to the trailer lighting. I completed the decorating theme with a red Santa hat, the kind with the white cotton ball on the pointy top, which I glued to a red baseball cap after affixing a "Mack Trucks" patch. I had wired the Santa-heads into the trailer's clearance light system, so when I flashed the clearance lights, Santa went off and on with the rest of the lights. The kids absolutely loved it, and a great many grown-ups did too. I nearly wore out the air horn, granting their requests to blow it.

One problem I never thought of when I decorated the truck was whether the decorations were legal. I never thought the pumpkins would be a problem, but I knew that a "by-the-book" DOT officer might take exception to Rudolph's red, light-up nose, since the regulations were clear about red lights belonging on the *back* of the truck. Still, I calculated, it's *Christmas*; surely the DOT wouldn't be Scrooge enough to object to such a small infraction. It didn't help when a driver traveling the other way opined on the C.B. that I would surely receive a ticket. In fact, several drivers made comments during the course of the week, predicting that the DOT would force me to remove either the red-nosed bulldog or the red-hatted Santa, or both. I had heard it enough times to be a little worried, but I stuck to my guns. "It's Christmas," I told everyone. "If the DOT wants me to remove the decorations, they'll just have to tell me themselves."

My resolve was tested one December dawn in Illinois. The C.B. radio warned that the State Police were setting up portable scales in the rest area on southbound I-55. (Never mind that "rest" areas should be used for *resting* and not for police enforcement activities. I'll try not to get started on *that*.) I knew that my truck was within legal weight limits, but there was a chance of an inspection. I was about to find out if the Illinois State Police were full of the Christmas spirit, or something else...

I pulled into the rest area to the sight of a dozen or more state troopers. The darkness was giving way to day, but it wasn't yet light enough to turn off the truck lights. They were just completing the set-up of the scales, and several were holding steaming cups of coffee as they watched me approach. Each one spoke to another, and by the time I pulled the truck onto the portable scales, they were *all* watching. And pointing. And smiling. And laughing. I couldn't help but think, "Yes, Virginia Trucker, there *is* a Santa Claus," as a trooper waved me back onto the highway.

47

My decorations were the biggest reason that I was sad to leave that tanker company. It just isn't the same with a big, white box for a trailer.

Today, when I see a truck with one of those strings of twelve twinkle lights and a plastic candy cane on the grill, I mentally thank them for remembering Christmas. I still have that bulldog, or "bulldeer," which is now mounted to a wooden base and wired to plug into the wall. It's a part of the family's annual Christmas decoration and it sits on the mantle instead of the hood, but it never fails to bring a smile from the kids. It still looks good, but, I remember when...

Chapter 10 - Instigating

Some days, things come at you fast and the time behind the wheel goes quickly. Other days are just plain boring. Sitting in the same seat for 10 hours, you could only listen to the "top 40" songs so many times, and the eyelids get heavy when mile after mile passes without some sort of mental stimulation. At times like these, I sometimes found the C.B. radio useful for instigating some lively entertainment over the airwaves.

Sometimes it was simple and easy. I'd simply make a sure-to-get-a-rise statement, like, "So-and-so is the best dang president we've ever had!" Nothing else was needed, as drivers from all over the political spectrum would chime in, and it wasn't long before heated discussion turned into nasty insults and threats of physical harm "if I ever find your 20!" (location).

Larry, a coworker in Atlanta, used a trick that I soon stole. It is common to hear only one side of a CB radio conversation, when the other party is out the range of your radio. Larry would pretend to be having such a conversation, advising someone that "it's 400 miles to Birmingham." Of course, less than 150 actual miles separate the two cities; a fact that other drivers would quickly point out. Undaunted, Larry would refute every comment, castigating the interrupter and using the most ridiculous logic imaginable. The argument would continue unabated for hours, and many local Atlanta drivers learned to tune in for the show. No matter how silly it got, there was always a driver or two who never figured out it was all in fun and left Atlanta still fuming at the stupidity of the guy that thought Birmingham was 400 miles away.

There was a time in Knoxville when I asked where a new guy in town could go for a good time. Except I asked the question with quite a lisp, generating a quick and angry response from an anti-gay local. "We don't allow your kind around here," said the voice. My lispy response, of course, was to praise him for his manly voice and ask him for a date. I suggested the carnival I had seen at a shopping center a ways back might be a good place to meet.

Growing angry, his insults gave way to threats of physical violence. "I'm gonna carry you up on Echo Mountain," he said, "and then I'm gonna throw you off!" I allowed that I might occasionally enjoy the rough stuff, especially if he was a handsome feller. It only seemed to spur him on. His signal alternated between strong and very weak as he cruised up and down the main drag searching for the object of his hatred, which happened to be me.

Of course, I wasn't ON the main drag, since I was securely parked on the Air Force Base waiting my turn to unload 7,000 gallons of jet fuel, but who am I to discourage such an entertaining, if bigoted, person?

Other drivers waiting to unload were thoroughly entertained, and we laughed all the way back to Atlanta.

My coup-de-grace had to be the day I lined 'em up on the Ohio Turnpike. On a beautiful summer day my eyes were drawn to the small foreign car going by in the fast lane. A young couple, maybe on vacation. The female passenger had an adorable little girl on her lap, standing up, holding on to Mama's thumbs as she bounced up and down, and laughing. She wore only a diaper in the summer air, long curly hair flying about as she bounced and giggled. As the car pulled ahead and the show ended, my mischievous plot was born.

"Break one-nine" I said into the CB microphone. "You ain't gonna believe this, but I just got passed by a young lady that didn't have on a *stitch* from the waist up!" "Where?" a driver demanded, and I gladly provided the direction and mile marker. "What's she look like?" was the next question. I described her huge smile and her apparent unconcern at her near-nudity. "I'm going the wrong way!" one driver wailed. "I'm not," another chimed in. "What's she riding in?" Cheerfully, I provided a description of the car. Then came two drivers arguing about getting out of one another's way. Before long, there must have been 10 or 12 drivers lined up ahead, eyes glued to their rear-view mirrors for a glimpse of the scantily-clad girl in the white Toyota. I couldn't help but smile as I awaited their commentary.

It didn't take long. It began with a string of curses and an accusation that I had lied to my fellow drivers. Me? The driver of the next truck to be passed put it into perspective. "No," he said. "He told absolutely the truth. She IS a young lady naked from the waist up. And she seems quite happy about it." "Well, he had me ready for a show, that's for sure," another said. "But not *that* kind of show!"

I waited for the comments to fade away, and then wished a great day to "all of you perverts" before turning off the CB. The remaining miles somehow went by faster.

51

Chapter 11 - What it's *Really* Like

If you're an experienced truck driver, you might want to skip this chapter. Or, you may choose to read it to see if I'm telling the real deal. I have no intention of writing a self-help manual for rookies or "wannabes;" there are tons of them already on the market. On the other hand, I feel that it would be a disservice not to share a little of my hard-won knowledge.

For starters, there are two statements that sum up driving a truck over the road. They are:

1. It's the most satisfying job in the world, and:

2. It positively sucks.

And, there you have it. Sometimes, as you're driving across America, the sun is shining, your favorite song is on the radio and the truck stop coffee you're drinking is just right. The scenery is spectacular and you just know that the bluebird of happiness is hovering right over your tractor, waiting to perch on your shoulder as soon as you stop. You *will* have days like that, followed by a real nice paycheck at the end of the week.

Unfortunately, things don't always go so well. Of course, there are traffic jams and police inspections and bad weather. There are inconsiderate motorists and road construction and traffic lights that somehow know you are approaching and turn red just to mess up your day. But, most people readily assume that those kinds of things are a part of the job and they accept them in stride. Those are the little things. The big things make or break a driving career. Here are a few:

The Family

Maybe there's a "significant other" in your life and, or children. Maybe your family is still Mom, Dad and Sis. Many drivers don't think about the impact that a career on the road will have on their family relationships. Sure, they did just fine when you were gone on that fishing trip for a whole week. But, you didn't come home for a day and a half and then go on *another* fishing trip, and another, and so on for months at a time.

Driving a truck over the road for a living isn't a temporary absence. It's a *lifestyle* change that will exact an emotional toll on everyone in your family, including you. Your wife may be perfectly capable of calling the plumber or getting the car fixed without your help, but when the kids are in bed and the tears come, you're not there. When you *do* get home, you'll want some home cooking and some quality time with the kids. You'll have a pile of dirty laundry and you might need to cut the grass and fix the toilet.

From your wife's perspective, you're gone all week. When you finally get home, she gets to do your laundry and cook a terrific meal for you while you play with the kids. If you're not sleeping, that is. She understands that you are tired from running all week and understands when your "intimate moment" is just that; a *moment*, followed by prolonged snoring. Trust me; that routine will get old when you repeat it week after week after week.

You

The routine will get old for you, too. You'll learn about Junior's first steps in a phone call that will likely get cut short by Junior squalling in the background. Your tender words to your partner will be heard by the truck drivers at the adjoining table as you try to speak softly into your cell phone. You'll find out quickly that you can't give a hug over the phone, or a kiss, or a handshake, or a spanking.

There is a well-known employment cycle that driver-recruiters are very familiar with. You're on the road for three weeks at a time and your family is suffering for it. You can't quit, because your family needs the money. So, you start looking for that job that will get you home every *two* weeks. When you find it, you jump. Then, you find one that gets you home *every weekend*, and you jump again. Then, you find out that "weekend" means you'll be getting home Saturday afternoon and leaving Sunday to make a Monday morning delivery. So, you jump to yet another company that promises a little more home time. On and on it goes, until you need three pages to record all of your previous employers on a job application. Down deep, you know the real answer is to get off the road, but you can't afford to quit.

If I could offer one piece of advice, it's this: Don't get so busy *making* a living that you can't *do* any living.

More Advice

OK, if I could offer *two* pieces of advice. Get the endorsements on your Commercial Drivers License. Get *all* of them, including Hazardous Materials. Why? Because, that CDL represents your professional credentials. The job you don't want *today* may be the job you must have *tomorrow*. The more endorsements you have, the greater your chances of finding work. Why *wouldn't* you be as qualified as you can be?

For example, if you're one of those drivers that finds you really need to be home on a daily basis, you will find that local truck-driving jobs don't pay as well as over the road positions. They don't *have* to, because they have plenty of drivers to choose from. The petroleum industry offers one local job that *does* pay well. Many gas stations need a delivery a day and sometimes multiple deliveries to supply the public. It goes without saying that drivers without Haz-Mat and Tanker endorsements can't be hired. But, even if you stay on the road, you'll find that many companies won't hire you without the HM endorsement or will pay you more if they do hire you.

Maybe you think you'll never drive a bus. I did, until my church pastor asked me to haul some kids to Sunday school. The Doubles-Triples endorsement helped me get another job, even though I had never pulled doubles. Get them all. You never know.

The Customers

Let's make this clear from the start. Customers are interested in your *trailer*. That trailer moves their freight to market or brings them product to sell or materials to make products to sell. They understand that a driver comes with the truck. So do oil drips and lug nuts. Some customers treat you like the professional you are. Others, well, see the aforementioned oil drips and lug nuts. There will be places where you aren't allowed on the dock. No rest rooms. No vending machines or water. Wait in your truck, please. Sometimes, you'll wait for a long, long time. It's not their problem if you lose a day's pay because you missed the appointment to pick up your next load.

Others provide you with a lounge, a TV, phones. Still others consider you to be free labor and your trailer to be free warehouse space. Object if you like, they have lots of other trucks to unload. My very favorite customer was a candy factory in Burlington, WI. Not only did they have a nice driver's lounge, but on those occasions when an errant forklift damaged a case of candy bars, they salvaged the good ones and put them in the lounge for the drivers. You could eat all you wanted, but you couldn't take any with you. I always wore my cargo pants with lots of pockets when I went there. I could probably fill another book with stories about my least favorite customers.

The Shower

Some people like to shower at night, before going to bed. Others like to shower when they first get up so they start the day clean and fresh. Truckers shower when they *can*. Well, most of them do. On the road, you'll be taking your showers in truck stops. Some of them are wonderful; clean, spacious and well appointed. Others, not so much. I left one place when I pulled back the shower curtain and saw cockroaches scurrying back into the drain when the light hit them. At another truck stop, I placed my bag with clean clothes underneath the sink so it would be out of the way while I shaved. I didn't know the drain pipe under the sink was broken and that every drop of my shaving water was draining onto my clean clothes. I learned to check the shower out carefully *before* I got naked. It was faster that way.

Truck stops charge for use of their shower rooms, and you'll pay anywhere from five dollars up to fifteen. However, most of them let you shower for free if you fill up your truck. The problem is that many companies use fuel optimization programs that *tell* you where to fuel up. Maybe you like the showers at the Taj Mahal Truck Stop, but your company sends you to Bubba's Fuel Emporium across the street. They save three cents a gallon on fuel, and you carefully check the shower for cockroaches.

You'll need to *plan* your showers when you're on the road. While you're planning the route you'll take and where you'll stop for the night, think about where you'll clean up, too. And, carry some disposable wipes to freshen up when you can't shower.

The Home Throne

You'll miss the home porcelain, too. On the road, every time you use the restroom, you'll be occupying a throne that a complete stranger left just moments before. Probably that big guy over there in the greasy-gray "athletic" pants. Betcha he's the guy that was so afraid of cooties that he used half a roll of tissue as a barrier between his considerable backside and the toilet seat and then tried to flush it all down. He's probably the guy that drew the "booger firing range" on the back of the stall door, too. (Note: use an individually-wrapped, disposable wipe to disinfect the seat.)

Clean Duds

Laundry will be a problem if you run out of clothes before you get home. I could make a pair of jeans last and I always packed extra socks and underwear, but I'd sometimes run out of shirts. There never seemed to be time to use the washer and dryer at the truck stop, so I'd end up buying those three-for-ten-dollars souvenir tee shirts. My poor wife never knew what she'd pull from the laundry bag. One of my prizes that I didn't check carefully had a large marijuana leaf printed on the back. Mostly, the shirts were cheap because they were factory seconds or misprints. Like the one that said "Flori" on the front and "da" in the armpit.

Meals

You'll spend $10 on meal, beverage and a tip every time you eat at a truck stop restaurant, and that's only if you don't order the expensive stuff. That's thirty dollars a day, two hundred and ten dollars a week. In a month's time you'll spend more on meals than you do on your mortgage payment, meaning you won't have enough money left to *make* your mortgage payment. If you'd rather take that money home, buy a cooler. Bring your own food, and buy something to heat it in. My wife would freeze leftovers in covered, plastic containers. They helped keep the cooler cold and provided home-cooked meals when I was a long way from home.

Trucks

As a new driver, you aren't going to get a brand-new truck. You'll get what's on the lot. It may stink of the last driver's cigarette smoke, pets, or even the last driver. It may have mechanical problems that the last driver didn't report as he or she left the company. It may not be your favorite color and it may not come with a kitchenette in the sleeper berth or a whirlpool bath nestled under the bunk. Here's what many drivers fail to understand; it's not a motor temple. It's a *tool* you use to make your living. I've seen drivers waste a whole day complaining about a spot on the carpet and some dirt on the fender. That's a day's pay lost. If it's important, meaning a health or safety issue or impacts your ability to make on-time delivery, by all means, get it fixed. Otherwise, get your dispatch and go. That's what they hired you for.

Dispatchers

Most companies call them Fleet Managers or Driver Managers. The act of *dispatching*; actually sending you someplace on a load, is generally only a small part of their duties. They are front-line supervisors who are responsible for the job you do. They are accountable for your mileage, on-time delivery, fuel efficiency, safety record and other variables. Dispatchers are your connection with the company and can make or break you. Take the time to cultivate a relationship with your dispatcher and your job will be much smoother.

A little-known fact; at many companies, the dispatcher does not choose the load that is assigned to you. "Load Planners" use computer programs to make the decision. They'll punch in the time and location that a customer's load will be available, and the computer provides a list of trucks that will be closest, what time they will be empty and how many hours they will have available to run. Some programs suggest the "best match" of load and available driver. Often, the load planner sends the load to the driver via the satellite communication system. You may know what your next dispatch is before your dispatcher does.

Your dispatcher knows things that the load planner may not be aware of, such as:

- He promised to do his best to get you home by the 12th.
- You've been to New York City twice this month already and it really isn't fair to send you there again.
- You mentioned that your truck is sluggish and you'd like to avoid a heavy load through the mountains until you can get it looked at.
- You've had two short runs in a row and need a longer run to get your miles up for a decent paycheck next week.

Your dispatcher can discuss your situation with the load planner to get you a different dispatch. Or, at least work to get you a good load to make up for the stinker you had yesterday. Do you really want to bite her head off?

Repairs

I once watched a driver quit because the shop wouldn't put new tires on his tractor. The technician carefully explained that the tires, although worn, had at least a few months of life left. They were legal, and they were safe. Then the Maintenance Manager got involved, explaining that tires are a company's second largest vehicle expense, after fuel. No company could afford to replace tires when they were still serviceable. The driver was having none of it; he was through. He retrieved his car from the parking lot and began loading his gear into it. Can you see this coming? His car was a rusted relic and at least two of the tires were not legal to drive on. I guess it was easier for him to spend the company's money than his own.

I am reminded of a driver I worked with at a company where I drove a petroleum tanker. "Stan" and I slip seated a tractor. He worked the night shift and handed the truck off to me at six in the morning. Except, he always had a list of mechanical problems to write up that never specified a real problem. He'd write up a "miss in the engine" or "lurching during a turn." Mechanics would waste hours trying to find the mystery defect while I waited in the driver's room for my truck.

One day as I waited I was approached by the shop manager. I never knew his real name; for some reason everyone simply called him "Stormy." Maybe that was his CB Radio "handle" in his trucking days. Stormy was perplexed. Stan had written up that the tractor "needed new shock absorbers." Stormy had personally inspected the shocks and found nothing wrong with them. "If I replace them," he told me, "I'll just be wasting money." "Fine," I told him. "Sign off on the paperwork and let me get to work. "If I don't replace the shocks," he said, "Stan will keep writing it up. What should I do?" he asked.

"Isn't it dark when Stan gets here to pick up the truck?" I asked. Since it was the time of year when days are short, it was. Stormy's eyes lit up when I told him to get a can of spray paint and put a fresh coat on the shock absorbers. "In the bad light," I suggested, "Stan will think he's looking at new shocks."

The following morning, Stan was late coming in from his shift and I met him at the fuel pump to take possession of the truck. "Truck running OK?" I asked. "Sure is," he said. "In fact, it's handling a lot better since they put those new shocks on. Take my advice," he continued, "don't let those mechanics get lazy on you. I stood my ground until they put on new shocks. Want to see?"

I told him I'd take his word for it.

Every company looks for ways to keep maintenance cost in line. Some, admittedly, take it too far. Most, however, will do what is necessary to keep your truck safe and legal. Keep in mind, however, that a tire purchased out on the road costs much more than the tires they have back in the garage. Remember, too, that there are unscrupulous repair facilities that overcharge for parts or even misrepresent the work that needs to be done. Does your truck really need a $1,400 radiator, or is it just low on anti-freeze? Is the weather cool enough that you can live without air conditioning for two days until you get back to a company terminal? Some expensive repairs are covered under the manufacturer's warranty, but must be repaired at a dealer to qualify. Don't break the law, and don't drive an unsafe truck. Outside of that, be a team player and help your company keep costs down when you can.

Chapter 12 - My Mack Truck

By today's standards, my '88 R-Model Mack was an object to be scorned. The three hundred horsepower engine provided barely enough power to move the truck out of its own way. Five speeds in the transmission was about half-enough. The cab was tiny and noisy. The average coffin has more space than the sleeper did, and going to bed was a process that included moving suitcases and everything else off the bed and into the cab to make room. It was attached by a large rubber gasket that would often leak. And the ride? It was rough enough to be legendary, but that's another chapter.

Despite her drawbacks, she was the first truck I had ever owned and will always have a special place in my memory. She was used when I bought her, and with her I learned the trucking business. She taught me many expensive lessons about the cost of purchasing and maintaining a truck. The engine was rebuilt when I wrecked her on a mountain in West Virginia, described in another chapter of this book. Piece by piece I replaced aging, broken parts; transmission, differential, brake drums, generators, tires, and so on. About the third repair, the service manager gave me a Mack™ tee shirt. I think he felt bad about the amount of money I was spending, but Mack had a series of shirts decorated with images of their namesake bulldog, and I was glad to get it. I liked the next one, too, and the one after, until I finally figured out that each tee shirt was costing me about $1,500 in tractor repairs.

Nothing gave me a bigger headache than the air conditioning. I could open the window when driving, of course, and there was a heavy-duty fan mounted on the dash. Back then, I could ride around with my shirt off without facing ridicule from passing motorists. But A/C was a necessity for sleeping during the day and sometimes at night, too. The shop at the dealer was crowded and I made appointments several days in advance, hoping the weather would be on the cool side until I got there. At the time, I ran a dedicated route that brought me past the dealer on a near-daily basis.

First, it was the evaporator, at about $1,200 to replace and recharge the system with Freon. After a few days, the cool air ceased, and the process started over; appointment, expensive repair, "free" tee shirt. Next was a $1,500 compressor. A few more days, and the condenser went. Back to the shop I went. I left $1,400 poorer, with another tee shirt and working air conditioning. I was confident that things would go better now, since virtually all the parts of the A/C system were brand-new. I sure needed a few repair-free weeks to recoup the money I had sunk into repairs. It was a good thing, too, since several days of 100-degree weather were predicted for the upcoming week.

It only took two days for the system to break again, and I wasn't happy. The shop was already closed for the day when it happened, but I knew I'd be back by there the following morning and I could sleep with the windows open tonight. I made a delivery in Peoria the next day, and called the dealer to tell them I'd be there in a couple of hours. "We're all booked up," the service manager said. "It'll be next week before we'll be able to get to you."

I tried to be nice; I really did. I explained that I had already spent more than four-thousand dollars on this problem and have the tee shirts to prove it. I pointed out that the weatherman was calling for extremely hot weather. I demanded that they stand by their repair work. Our conversation was tense, but cordial; until he informed me that he "had problems of his own." "What?" I said. "Next week," he replied, and hung up the phone. I was hot when I arrived at the dealership, partly from the weather, and I was in no mood for pleasantries.

I didn't mention that this particular dealership was in a rather unique situation. The lease had expired on their old dealership location, and the new one wasn't yet ready to move in. In the interim, they had set up a temporary location in a rented warehouse. It worked fine, except that there was only one door into the garage. That's the one I parked right in the middle of. The service manager ran up, and I *think* he was saying that I couldn't park there, but I didn't hear it. Whatever he said was lost is the large "whoosh" of air that sounded when I set the parking brake.

Or, maybe it was drowned out by the long blast of the air horn I gave them to announce my presence. I exited the truck with keys in hand and heard, "What the *hell* are you doing?" The man seemed rather agitated. "I'm waiting for my air conditioner to be fixed," I replied. "I told you it would be next week," he stated adamantly. "Now, move that truck!" I sounded calmer than I felt when I answered. "That truck moves when the air conditioner is blowing cold air, and not one second before." I told him. "Unless you think you can get these keys from me." I leaned in with a glare, just for emphasis.

The dealership general manager burst from his office to intervene. After a brief conversation that the service manager didn't appear to enjoy, he promised that if I gave him the key, the truck would be moved to a service bay and someone would begin work immediately. A couple of hours later, he let me know that the problem had been an inexpensive "O" ring that should have been replaced along with all the other parts. "No charge," he said, offering a tee shirt. "No, thanks," I told him. "I've got quite a collection already."

I will mention one very unique feature of my Mack that I designed and installed myself. I absolutely *hated* the Illinois 55 mile-per-hour speed limit for trucks. When they passed a law banning radar detectors in commercial vehicles, I felt it was too much to take. My little Mack might have a top speed of 62, but I wanted *all* of it. Maybe the fact that I owned a $250 radar detector helped to sway my opinion. At any rate, I carefully planned my modification and then I bought the parts. I created a "bird-dog box;" a retractable space for the radar detector. With the flip of a switch, what appeared to be a speaker on the dashboard rose up about 3 inches, revealing the radar detector beneath. Another flip and it all disappeared. It was brilliant, and virtually undetectable; something that might have been seen in a James Bond movie.

Years later, when I sold the truck, the buyer was very non-committal as he inspected every last detail of the used tractor. He asked a ton of questions, remaining stone-faced through it all. Finally, he climbed behind the wheel for a test drive. We were nearly back to our starting point when he noticed an unlabeled switch and asked what it was for. "Go ahead, flip it," I said. His eyes widened as my secret accessory rose from the dash, and for the first time, he smiled. He paid full price.

Chapter 13 - Lot Lizards

The majority of truck drivers are men, and professions that employ lots of men naturally attract businesses that are geared towards the masculine gender, such as prostitution. Of course, I had heard stories from instructors and drivers, even before graduation from CDL School. I had seen the "no lot lizard" decal some drivers put on their tractors, so I wasn't completely uniformed. But still, somehow, the only "hookers" I had ever seen were on T.V. I'll say this before I relate my experience with working girls (no, not *that* kind of experience); I mostly treated them with respect, whether I agreed with their choice of profession or not.

The first time I encountered lot lizards, I had made a stop at the old Union 76™ truck stop in South Holland, IL. Sitting in my truck, I observed four or five squad cars roll up to the front of the store, lights flashing in the night. Each cruiser was equipped with a spotlight, and those spotlights were now raking back and forth across the truck parking area. New to trucking, I assumed I was witnessing a drug bust, or maybe a roundup of illegal immigrants. But, soon, I noticed that the sweeping spotlights were *low*, shining beneath the parked trailers. They weren't looking for trucks; they were looking for people. And then, I noticed *legs*. Bare legs. *Girl* legs. Lots of them, running every-which-way. It was like someone caught the cheerleading squad passing a cigarette around, and they were all bailing. I never saw a police officer actually get out of the car; and I never saw any of the running girls above the waist, but I finally figured out what I was witnessing. The cops were simply scaring the girls away for a while. I suspected they would soon be back.

My first actual *encounter* with a prostitute was at a rest area in Pennsylvania. Just before climbing into the bunk, I spread my road atlas over the steering wheel to double-check my route for the following morning. I saw her walking from her car towards the truck. I assumed that her car was broken. Maybe she needed some help, or some directions; or maybe a couple of dollars. As she approached, I rolled down the window of the cabover tractor I had just parked. "Do you need some help, Ma'am?" I naively asked. "Would you like some company?" was her response. "No, thank you," I said, stupidly assuming that she was asking if she could ride along. "I'm fixing to lay it down for the night," I explained. Her reply made it all clear to me. "I know," she said. "I thought maybe you didn't want to lay down *alone*."

This is going to sound mean, but my first impression was that she was *ugly*. Her biceps looked to be as big around as my thighs, and from the jiggle I knew it wasn't muscle. Her top didn't make it all the way to her shorts, revealing a large expanse of whitish fat roll. Today, I think they call that a "muffin top," but in her case it was the whole dang cake She was wearing bright red shorts of some kind of stretchy material that must have been industrial-strength to contain the mass within. Her hair was door-knob brassy-blond and it appeared that her latest styling might have been at the mercy of someone's weed-whacker.

When I thought she was a lady in distress, of course, none of that mattered. After all, I'm no male model myself. But, honestly, I couldn't help but be astounded that she thought someone would actually *pay* for her services. I'm glad I stopped myself before I asked, and I stammered a polite, "No thank you, Ma'am." She asked if I was sure and I assured her I was; hoping that my face didn't reveal what I felt inside. Then I watched her walk away; bright-red industrial-strength shorts undulating with each heavy step. She turned back to look once, and I quickly averted my gaze and studied every minute detail of my road atlas until I was sure she wasn't coming back.

For some reason, I-94 between Chicago and Detroit seemed to attract a lot of business from the "ladies." Of course, I'd always hear them on the C.B. Radio around Hammond, Indiana, advertising their "company" to the passing drivers. Some of them had rehearsed presentations that almost sounded like a regular radio commercial, as if they were selling motor oil or something. I kind of resented the fact that they tied up the channel on the radio, but I usually paid them little mind. One, however, was very persistent; no one else could have a conversation for her constant interruptions to solicit business. Finally, one night I lost my patience. Picking up the microphone, I asked the young lady if she was running any "specials." She responded by asking what I meant. I said, "You know, like *two* venereal diseases for the price of one?" I shouldn't have done it, and she told me so in rather colorful terms, but, hey, it shut her up for a while.

One of the ladies broke my heart. At a rest area on I-94, I came out of the men's room and walked back to the truck in a downpour. Trying to stay as dry as possible, I walked quickly, and was about to climb into the cab when she asked if I needed some company. She stepped out of the area behind the tractor parked next to mine, where she had sought shelter from the rain. She looked to be about fourteen; a beautiful young lady, absolutely drenched, shivering from the cold rain. About the same age as my own daughter. "Go home, girl," I told her.

"This isn't what you want to do with your life." I had a hard time getting to sleep that night.

There were others, over the years, but most simply asked if I needed company and faded from memory soon after I respectfully declined. But I still remember a couple of them. Montgomery, Alabama has a well-known truck stop at the convergence of I-65 and I-185 where I was approached by a particularly-bold business woman. I had dropped my trailer and pulled to the door of the service bay to have a drive-tire repaired. There wasn't room in the garage, but the technician wheeled the jack out to the tractor and put it to use. As he removed the tire, I felt her come up beside me. "Need some company?" she asked. I should have simply declined, but I was struck by her apparent indifference to the sight of my tractor up on the jack right in front of us. "That's my truck," I told her, pointing to the tractor. "Oh, that's OK," she said. "What I meant," I said, "was they're fixing a tire on my truck. Where," I asked, "would we go, assuming that I *did* need some company?" "It's OK," she repeated. "We can just use your truck, anyway. I know these guys," she explained. I had this mental image of my truck bouncing wildly, driver and prostitute conducting business in the sleeper berth, while a technician was right outside, nonchalantly changing a tire. I politely thanked her and declined her offer...

The only other memorable encounter with the working ladies was, again, at a rest area on I-94. I was way behind schedule for an 8:00 a.m. delivery in Detroit. When I pulled into a rest area outside the city, I had time for only a few hours of sleep at most. It would be more of a "nap" than a night of sleep. It wasn't much, but it would have to do.

The tiny sleeper behind my R-Model Mack had an emergency door right next to my pillow. That's what the young lady knocked on shortly after I drifted off to sleep. Apparently, they had figured out that if they didn't see the driver in the cab of the tractor, the sleeper would be the place to target. After declining her offer of "company," I rolled over and went back to sleep.

It wasn't very long before I heard it again; tap, tap, tap on the sleeper door. "Persistent," I thought as I opened it again. A *different* young lady graciously offered *her* company as well. I politely declined her offer, too. I don't know how long it took to go back to sleep, but I was a little irritated about being woke up twice in a too-short night of sleep.

Tap, tap, tap. "Again?" I thought. I opened the door one more time; a *third* woman asked if I needed "company." I stuck my head out of the door and looked around. "How many trucks do you think are parked in this rest area?" I asked my would-be service provider. "I don't know," she said, "Maybe eight?" "Well," I said, "that's *three* girls for *eight* trucks in less than *three* hours. *Just how horny do you think we are?!!*"

No one bothered me during the last twenty minutes of my rest, but I couldn't go back to sleep.

Chapter 14 - Cats

If you're a dog person, you might want to skip this chapter. I love dogs, too, and my boxer puppy is curled at my feet as I write this, noisily chewing on her rawhide bone. But, this chapter is about cats. There are two that have entered my life entirely because of my career in trucking.

One of the runs I made frequently was to a foundry in New Brighton, Pennsylvania. Pulling a pneumatic tanker, I hauled sand that was used to make molds for casting iron parts; I never did find out what the products were. There were no truck stops nearby, and I often visited the employee's lunch room for a cold drink or snack while the trailer was being unloaded. The place was old and dingy and sand was everywhere, and there were cats. *Lots* of cats. If I estimated that fifty of them roamed the factory, I'd probably be pretty close. They were everywhere, and they'd scurry out of my way as I walked to and from the truck. Except for one small gray one. This one would run ahead to a point directly in my path, and then lie down on its side, mewing as I approached. If I walked around or stepped over, it would merely run past me and lie down again. "Friendly," I thought, giving it a couple of pats on the head.

I seldom ate my meals in truck stop restaurants, and so carried a supply of groceries with me. My food box included canned tuna as a source of quick protein. The cats looked hungry to me, and I opened a can of tuna and dumped it out on the sandy floor of the foundry. I was swarmed by cats, and the tuna disappeared in a matter of seconds. My little gray friend was too late to get any, so I opened another can, and then another.

Each week brought another delivery to New Brighton, and another can or two of tuna to the resident cats, who it seemed were getting to know me. The little gray one was always first to greet me, but the others were never far behind. The cats came to expect our little visits, or at least the tuna, and actually learned to recognize the sound of my truck. It was common to see ten or more on sitting on the concrete dock, drawn by the sound of my loaded tractor-trailer crawling up the steep hill to the plant.

During one of my deliveries, a foreman told me that the cat problem was getting out of hand at the foundry. He said the superintendent was concerned that cats were causing an unsanitary condition and might even cause safety problems by getting in and around the plant machinery. He announced that the order had been given to poison the cats; they would not be there the next time I returned.

While my trailer was unloaded, I agonized over the news. I could take some home, but we already had a cat. Truth is, I am allergic to cats anyway. I don't break into hives when I see one, but I always wash my hands after handling them. Rubbing an eye was sure to cause redness and discomfort, and my sinuses will still close down in a minute if I don't wash off their scent. This situation was different, however. These cats would die, and I felt terrible about it. By the time my trailer was empty, I had made up my mind; I couldn't save them all, but I would save at least one. The little gray one. I told the foreman of my plan and he encouraged me to take as many cats as I'd like. "No," I said, "just the little gray one."

We stopped at a shopping center on the way out of town and I got her a collar, a litter box and litter, some food and a couple of small dishes. She took to it like she was born to truck; maybe because she was already used to the noise and vibration of the plant machinery where she came from. It was comical how she would walk back and forth on the dash, mewing at each passing car as if they would stop and offer some tuna if they but saw her. However, I was a mess by the time we got home a week later. Being in such close proximity, my allergy kicked in with a vengeance, and I couldn't always wash my hands after I stroked her back or removed her from the dash. In fact, my eyes were swollen and purple, and it took a while to convince my wife that I hadn't been in a fight somewhere.

When I returned to the foundry a week later, the number of cats was greatly reduced, but they were still around. "I thought they were going to be poisoned," I told the foreman. "Aw, the superintendant says that about once a year," he replied, sheepishly. "Everybody starts taking them home to save them, and we keep the population down."

The kids loved the cat, naming her "Cleo." She was a part of our family for 18 years, never failing to respond to the sound of a can opener.

My other rescued cat never rode in a tractor trailer, but she was born underneath the double-wide trailer that was the office of the trucking company where I worked. Through a gap in the skirting under the trailer, we could hear her and her sisters mewing, and we often saw her calico mother leaving to hunt in the fields behind. I had no intention of taking a kitten, but then I hadn't intended to bring home a cat from a Pennsylvania foundry, either.

Late one evening, I let our dog out in the yard so she could take care of her business before we went to bed. I heard a plaintive mewing; a cry, really, coming from the direction of my pickup truck. I took my flashlight to investigate, but the mewing stopped each time my footsteps crunched the gravel of the driveway. I looked all around and under the truck, but found nothing. I assumed that a neighbor's cat was lurking in the vicinity, hoping it went home before I left for work in the morning.

The following morning, there was no sound coming from the area of the truck. I intentionally stamped my feet in the gravel as I walked all around, intending to scare off any animals that might be hiding beneath. Satisfied, I headed for work. My route included twenty or so miles of two-lane, country road, and traffic was always light this time of the morning. I always seemed to go a little faster than the 55 mph speed limit, and I was cruising along nicely at about 70, or maybe it was 75, when I heard the first heart-stopping scream.

I knew it was a cat, but the sound it made wasn't the mewing I had heard the night before. This was a scream, as if it had been run over or seriously hurt, or maybe frightened. My first thought was that it had somehow gotten into the engine compartment and got caught in a fan belt. I screeched to a halt and got out, looking first for a wounded animal in the road. I looked for fur, for blood, anything that might indicate the presence of an animal. It had sounded as if the animal were *in* the truck. I searched everywhere, under the hood, under the truck; even underneath the seats in case it had somehow gotten inside. I found nothing. Whatever it was, I reasoned, it must have run off into the woods beside the road.

I had just resumed cruising speed when I heard it again. Once more, I stopped and searched everywhere in and around the truck. I listened intently, just in case. No cat, nowhere. I repeated the sequence a third time when I heard the next scream. I was totally mystified by the horrible noise, and sure I was causing some poor animal incredible anguish, but try as I might I found nothing.

I kept my speed to about 30 mph and pulled up to the truck repair shop next door to the office where I worked. "There's a cat in my truck," I told the mechanic, who wore a shirt with "Joe" embroidered over the pocket. I told him the story, and he searched the pickup carefully, even sliding underneath on a creeper. "Whatever it was," Joe said, "it's gone now." Reluctantly, I drove over to the office, performing a quick U-turn when the poor thing sounded again. "Get in," I told the startled mechanic. I hit a speed bump, the cat screamed, and Joe said, "You got a cat in your truck." We returned to the garage.

He searched again, finding nothing. Then he announced that he had an idea, and disappeared into the shop office. He returned seconds later, followed by a small dog, which he encouraged to circle the pickup. On the third lap, the dog stopped at the right front wheel, and began sniffing the plastic wheel well inside the fender. Joe investigated, and then he bent back the pliant wheel well. His other hand disappeared behind the plastic liner, and reemerged holding a tiny ball of calico fur. "Guess you *did* have a cat in your truck," he cleverly remarked.

I found a box at the office, threw an old towel in the bottom, and put her in. To my chagrin, she cried each time I stepped out of her sight. It's a little embarrassing, trying to teach a classroom full of truck drivers while your kitten is calling for

79

you, but I managed. I cut a small hole in the side of the box and put it on a table in the classroom so that she could see me, and went back to work. A check by the veterinarian revealed only a couple of minor scrapes from her adventure.

Isabella has been with our family for eleven years, so far. I often have to shoo her from the desktop when I write.

Chapter 15 - Poor Boy & the Dixie Twister

Running jet fuel from Atlanta to Knoxville four or five times a week is about as gravy of a job as you'll find in trucking. But it does get monotonous. Unless you're running with a couple of drivers like Poor Boy and Twister. They'd get me laughing so hard I could hardly see to drive.

There was the time Poor Boy couldn't figure out why all those people passing him were pointing and laughing. He couldn't see the pair of pantyhose Twister had tied to the ladder on the back end of his tanker. Traveling down the highway, the pantyhose had caught the wind stream and inflated, billowing out behind the trailer and providing great entertainment to the motoring public. Except Poor Boy, who finally found them when he pulled over to see for himself what was so funny.

Of course, payback came in short order, when Twister finished loading and refused to wait for Poor Boy because he allegedly had a rendezvous planned with his latest conquest. Twister considered himself a womanizer and talked incessantly about his exploits. Once he introduced Poor Boy and me to his current flame, who was considerably less attractive than his embellished accounts had led us to believe. Poor Boy nearly tripped as he backed away quickly. "Twister," I told him later, "if you aren't going to have any morals, you ought to at least have some standards."

On this occasion, Twister stayed at the loading facility just long enough to brag that his latest "little darlin'" was meeting him on the shoulder of the ramp to Airport Road. There was no time to waste; he had to go. Poor Boy finished loading and followed about 15 minutes behind, just out of CB range.

It wasn't long before he heard someone on the CB you wouldn't want your children to hear. A homosexual prostitute was advertising for some business, which hatched a plot in Poor Boy's mind. He struck up a conversation. "Where can we meet?" the enterprising business-person asked, and Poor Boy closed the deal. "I'll be waiting at the Airport Road exit," he said, providing a perfect description of Twister's truck. "I don't have much time," he said, urgently. "I'll be there in five-minutes," came the reply. "Hurry!" said Poor Boy. Twister didn't speak to Poor Boy for nearly a week after the wrong "little darlin'" showed up.

My turn came the night Poor Boy swerved to avoid a deer on the edge of the highway. Which was really a big clump of grass. For miles, Twister and I tried to convince him to see an eye doctor. For his own safety, we warned him of every mailbox, trash bag, or other item that he might mistake for a deer. Finally, Poor Boy announced that he had spotted a REAL deer, and before either of us had seen it. "No way" I said. He told us where to look, and sure enough, there was a deer standing in the yard, alongside a trailer house. But it was a plastic target deer; one of those with parts you could replace after you shot it full of holes. Poor Boy insisted it was real.

"Yankee," he called me, "don't you have deer up North?" The good natured back and forth continued until Poor Boy issued the challenge. "If that's a fake deer," he said, "it'll still be there when we come back this way." I allowed as how that was true. "Well, I say it's real, and it will be gone." "You're on," I told him. "Granny's best sausage biscuit," he said, wagering the breakfast specialty at our favorite stop in Maryville. "And coffee," I added. "Bring your billfold, Yankee," was his reply.

It was gone. I don't know how he did it but hours later, when we came by on the return trip, the target deer was gone. I accused him of subterfuge, but nothing I said would budge him from his claim that a live deer had simply moved on. Poor Boy relished his victory for a whole week. At Granny's, he refused to let me get the check, claiming the joy of knowing I owed him was worth prolonging the wait for his prize. When I could stand it no longer, I told him, "Today's your last chance. I'm ordering your sausage biscuit and paying off my debt." And I did. While Poor Boy was still in the Men's room, I called our favorite waitress over and placed the order. "How small can Granny make a biscuit?" I asked, telling her about our wager.

She returned with two saucers and a strange smile. In front of me, she placed a biscuit so large that it obscured the saucer, with what appeared to be a half-pound of steaming pork sausage protruding from the sides. Every eye in the restaurant watched her bring it, and Poor Boy's eyes lit up at the sight.

With a flourish, she placed Poor Boy's breakfast on the table. You could have hidden Poor Boy's biscuit under a quarter, it was so small. I can't repeat Poor Boy's comment, but the tables were turned as the entire restaurant erupted in laughter. "I got this," I announced, and went to the register, check and billfold in hand. "I always pay my debts." I said.

Poor Boy was so mad he refused to eat the second biscuit she brought out, just as large as mine.

Chapter 16 - Getting Hired

I don't know how many times I have heard a driver describe a former employer by saying, "They *blackballed* me!" Another way I've heard it said is, "They *DACed* (pronounced "dacked," rhymes with whacked) me." With years of experience on each side of this equation, I have learned a few things about the process. Unless you have one of the cushy, union line-haul jobs, statistics say that you will change employers at some point during the next year. What you read here might help you do that.

Almost every company of any size gives you a copy of the Federal Motor Carrier Safety Regulations during orientation. Usually, it's a pocket-sized booklet about an inch thick. It's the one you lost, threw away, tossed in the storage area in the sleeper, or otherwise disposed of unless you happen to be in the small minority of CDL drivers who actually *read* it.

There's a reason they gave you the book. Well, there are *reasons*. There's the altruistic one; they care about you and want you to be fully informed, complying with all legal requirements while operating as safely as possible. The other reason is that when they need to fire you for violating the regulations, they'll have that little receipt you signed that guarantees you won't get away with, "I didn't know..."

Read the book, especially if you are new to the industry. Knowledge is power, but not if it's in the storage area under your bunk. You'll find a lot of information in there about your relationship with your employer. Things like what they can and can't do when it comes to drug testing, or what documents they are required to keep in your file. And, what they are required to check when they hire you.

Obtaining or Disputing Your Background Reports

The regulations (FMCSRs) mandate that prospective employers must conduct a background check on every driver they hire. The first step that most carriers will take is to order reports on your background. For a few important reasons, you should *know* what your background reports will show, so that you are aware of what the company you have applied to will see.

• If information shows up on your background that you did not disclose up front, it may be assumed that you were not completely honest in the recruiting process, and the company may decide to go no further.

• On the other hand, some companies will report things that others won't. For example, that tire you curbed back in Cincinnati? One company won't mention it. Another will report it as a full-blown accident. You need to know so you are prepared.

• You have the legal right to dispute the information in your reports and to have the information removed if it isn't correct. But, you have to see it to know if you need to contest it.

It isn't difficult to find out what's being reported about your background, and you should do it before you begin your search for a new job, if you can. This chapter describes some of the reports commonly used and tells you how to obtain them.

Motor Vehicle Report (MVR)

By law, every company you apply to must obtain your Motor Vehicle Report (MVR) showing your driving record for at least the past 3 years. Each state differs, however, on what is reported. Some only show information for 3 years, while others report back to the date you first obtained your license. I've seen five-page reports from Pennsylvania that go back to that speeding ticket you got in high school. Some show only traffic citations, while others show accidents, incidents, child support issues, criminal convictions and other information. Contact your state's Department of Motor Vehicles or Public Safety Department to order this report in your state and in any other states where you held a license during the past 3 years. And if you got a ticket that didn't show up on your MVR, don't even *think* about not disclosing it. Your company is required to order a new report annually, and when that ticket finally shows up, you'll likely be fired. You don't want "falsified employment application" on your DAC report, which we discuss next.

"DAC" Report

Although "DAC Report" is the term most commonly used, this report is actually a history of your employment maintained by a company called HireRight in Tulsa, OK. Not every company reports your work history to HireRight, and not every company you apply to will order a report from them. However, nearly *all* of the larger companies will do both. It's a convenient one-stop source for much of the information they are required to obtain. Most companies that order your employment history also order other reports from HireRight. Here's a list of the most common:

- CDLIS – shows ALL Commercial Driver's Licenses you have held in the past 3 years.

- Employment History – shows information *reported* by previous motor carrier employers.

- Criminal History – shows arrest and conviction information for states and counties you have lived in. Each county reports differently. Some drivers find that an offense from many years ago is still on their record, while others are surprised when a recent offense isn't listed.

HireRight is a "consumer reporting agency," which means your rights are covered under the same laws as the credit report your lender might obtain. You have the right to see what is being reported about you. Here's how (current November, 2011):

Write them at:
HireRight
Attn: Consumers Department
P.O. Box 33181
Tulsa, OK 74153

Online at:www.hireright.com/Consumers-Applicants.aspx.

Or call them at (800) 381-0645.

You should receive your reports within 15 days. Be sure to write down your case number. If you disagree with information on your background reports, there are a couple of things you can do. The law (FMCSRs) says you have three basic rights. 1)To see the information, 2)To dispute the information, and 3) To have your rebuttal statement included with the information when it is given to prospective employers. HireRight has a process for disputing the information in your work history and will include your rebuttal in their report if you wish.

To dispute other information, you'll need to go to the source. For example, if a company turns you down, you have 30 days to request (in writing) all the documentation they used to make their decision and they must provide the documents within 5 business days. Suppose your last employer, XYZ Trucking, reported that you abandoned a truck. You dispute that because you followed the instructions of the night dispatcher, who told you to leave your truck in Dallas. Your regular, daytime dispatcher wanted that truck in Albuquerque and wasn't happy about the Dallas thing, so she reported a truck abandonment to your record. In addition, she was counting on you taking a load to Chicago even though she hadn't told you about it yet. You left her in a bind when you quit, so she reported "quit under dispatch," too.

In this case, contact your old company – in writing – telling them that you dispute the report and ask them to correct it. Don't send your request to the dispatcher; send it to the Safety Director or Manager. If they refuse to correct your record, write up your rebuttal statement and send it to them. Avoid the name calling and the anger issues; just state the facts. They may correct your record. Even if they don't, the next time they verify your employment, they must include your rebuttal statement.

To dispute information on your MVR, contact your state Department of Motor Vehicles. If criminal information is reported erroneously, contact the county that reported it. And, to correct information on your PSP report, contact the FMCSA and follow their procedures.

Pre-Employment Screening (PSP)

This report came into being with the new CSA requirements, and is widely misunderstood. It also, unfortunately can be extremely unfair to the driver, and I have devoted an entire chapter to that subject elsewhere in this book. Information on your PSP is compiled from the system used by the police officer when you are stopped for a citation or inspection. A prospective employer knows when and where you were stopped, *why* you were stopped, and what the results were. It is very possible that a driver with a squeaky clean MVR and an impeccable work history can be denied a job because if information in the PSP report.

Know what is in yours. It will cost you $10, and you can order it online at: www.psp.fmcsa.dot.gov/psp/default.aspx. You'll find the process to dispute your report here as well.

Employment Gaps

Employers are required to check periods when you didn't have a job for more than thirty days, too. Partly, this to verify that you weren't in jail or attending a terrorist training camp while you weren't working. Partly, it's to make sure you didn't have a truck wreck while working for a company you didn't mention in your application. And, partly, a lot of unemployment time can be an indicator of a poor work ethic. Be prepared to explain periods of unemployment.

Please, don't claim you were "looking for a job." Trucking companies are always screaming for drivers. You weren't looking very hard if you couldn't find a trucking job in 10 months! My favorite is, "I quit to take care of my poor, sick grandmother. I'm sure it's possible that you were the only person she could count on, but it's hard for me to understand how being unemployed and sponging off of Granny helps to make her last days better.

Leaving, the Right Way

The best way to ensure that your employment history will reflect favorably upon your record is to leave a company the right way. Too many drivers let anger cloud their best judgment when they leave. It may be inconvenient to return the truck to a specified terminal, but most carriers are quick to report an abandoned vehicle, especially if a customer's load was abandoned, too.

Never use your employer's truck as your taxi home either, unless your company approves. It's inconvenient to be stuck in the middle of nowhere with a sleeper full of personal belongings. But, many companies will deduct the expense of the extra 500 miles you drove from your last paycheck and will put "unauthorized use of company funds" on your record if you burned the fuel they purchased for your trip to the house.

I received a call from one particular driver who was incensed that our company had put "misuse of company funds" on his work history report. He had driven the truck nearly a thousand miles off-route to his home, which was far from any company terminal. He wasn't concerned about the customer, who needed the load he had been dispatched to deliver. He wasn't very sympathetic when I told him he had burned over six hundred dollars worth of the company's fuel. He didn't really care that he had rung up a couple of hundred dollars worth of tolls on the electronic toll transponder in his tractor. He didn't want to hear about the hundreds of dollars it would cost to send someone to pick up the tractor and trailer. He certainly didn't care about the cost of getting the unit out of the impound lot, where it had been towed after he abandoned it at the closed-down Wal-Mart. He just wanted to know why we had "blackballed" him. Go figure.

I know, I know, if you tell them you're quitting, they'll dispatch you everywhere *but* home in an effort to keep you from leaving. Undoubtedly, there are some companies or dispatchers who will do just that. But, if you give a notice and are professional about the way you leave, most companies will work with you to get you and your belongings to your home. They'll be less inclined to put bad information in your work history. And, they'll be more likely to hire you back if you need a job in the future.

When I was training for my first recruiting job, a crusty old-timer put it this way: "I can," he said, "tell a heck of a lot more about a driver from the way he leaves a job than from how he starts one." That's good to remember.

Chapter 17 - The Passenger

Many of my memories of the road are pleasant, but one still haunts me. I won't forget one January Illinois night when my pride in my fellow drivers was turned to shame. Weather reports were grim; a shift in the Jet Stream brought cold Arctic air to the Midwest. New records for cold were predicted, perhaps 25-below with a wind-chill of 60-below or worse. Radio stations warned that exposed skin would freeze in seconds. It was best to stay indoors. But I had taken the right precautions and the truck was running well with the cab toasty warm.

As I crossed I-80 the radio announced that a new record had, indeed, been set. I kept an ear to the C.B. too, for the latest weather developments or just in case someone called for help. Some time after midnight I overheard two drivers discussing a pedestrian they had spotted on the shoulder of the Interstate. One mentioned the deadly cold and the folly of being out in it, while the other announced his intention to stop and offer help. Only, he didn't. After a long silence, the first driver asked if he had stopped. "I was gonna," he said. "Until I saw that it's a," well, I'm not going to say it. The person in danger was African-American, and the driver didn't allow that kind in his truck, period. The other driver responded with some gibberish about his company's no-passenger policy and the two went on into the night.

Incensed, I didn't need a heater to stay warm as I picked up the microphone to share my thoughts with the bigoted cowards.

But, before I could speak, I saw the old Buick on the shoulder, left-front tire folded up underneath as if it was a broken toy. Snow was already beginning to drift around it, propelled by winds howling across the fields that bordered the highway. I saw no one in or around the car, and I somehow knew it was the source of the pedestrian the drivers had been discussing.

I strained to see the driver walking in the night and soon did. No hat. No gloves. No scarf or boots or earmuffs. A thin person wearing a thin jacket against the cold. I threw on the four-ways and came to a stop beside – her. A teenage girl in a High School jacket, nearly frozen and scared to death. Somebody's daughter, sister. She remained silent when I spoke to her from the opened passenger door, weighing the risk of climbing into a stranger's truck against certain death from the cold. As gently as I could, I convinced her climb up into the truck.

She sat with her back to the door, curled up and still scared, never taking her eyes off of me. After a while, I got her to speak, but only a few words. I said I planned to get off at the first exit with a business where she might find a pay phone and keep warm until her folks arrived. She shook her head, slightly, in agreement. But the restaurant we found was closed and there was no pay phone outside. So was the gas station at the next exit. We found an open convenience store one exit further, but the rough-looking group hanging around the parking lot frightened her worse than I did. So I made a decision. Likely illegal, maybe unsafe, undoubtedly stupid. I took her home.

With few soft words and hand gestures, she directed me to an older residential neighborhood in Joliet with narrow streets and old houses and cars parked on both sides of the street. At each intersection I'd stop and wait for her to point the direction. A couple of turns were too tight and I'm sure more than one resident woke up to find truck tracks in the snow across a corner of their yard. But she finally said, "Here," and I stopped the truck. I offered coat, gloves, blanket, money, but she only shook her head and slowly backed down the steps to the ground. And then, without a word, she disappeared.

I never saw which house she went to, or if she went off somewhere between the houses to somewhere else. I wanted to believe that worried parents greeted her with hugs and tears of joy and relief. But I'll never know. She could have been a runaway, a criminal, a – well, it doesn't matter. She wasn't a frozen corpse on the side of I-80, and that will have to be enough.

When I finally shut down, I lay awake for a long time, pondering those frightened, brown eyes, and two men with hearts colder than the Arctic air.

Chapter 18 - Traffic Cones

I hate 'em. Those orange traffic cones never mean anything good. They mean construction. They mean slow. They mean, "You can't go there." For being such flimsy little things, they sure cause a lot of trouble.

There was the town in Ohio where the local community college was holding some sort of Saturday-morning event. I have long forgotten what it was, but traffic was brutal. When I got close to the event, I discovered that everyone in the right lane was supposed to turn right, directly into the event parking area. Except, the geniuses who were directing traffic had neglected to put up any warning signs in advance of the intersection. Not one. I arrived at the intersection to see a beautiful arc of new orange cones, starting at the dashed line on my left and forming a gracefully curved lane into the entrance drive on my right. A stern looking rent-a-cop waved me to the right. One look told me all I needed to know; there was no way I was pulling a tractor-trailer into that parking lot. The likelihood of getting the big truck out without damage to several autos was miniscule. I couldn't change lanes, and I wasn't going to turn right. I would have happily explained it all to the guy directing traffic, until he blew his whistle and, with a nasty scowl, gestured wildly for me to go to the right. "Sorry," I thought, "Not happening." Blip! Blip! Blip! The cones fell as I drove right over them. I saw the rent-a-cop, still waving in my west-coast mirror as I continued on my way. I don't remember, but I think I might have waved back.

I remember being stuck in a long line of traffic in a construction zone on I-55. The one southbound lane of traffic wasn't moving at all, and it didn't help that the northbound side seemed to be flowing smoothly. I found entertainment value, however, in watching the workers scramble to stand the cones back up after some errant motorist knocked one or two down. The entertainment peaked, however, when a trucker pulled a 14-foot wide mobile home section through the 12-foot wide lane. One by one, the cones fell. Blip, blip, blip. One construction worker angrily scrambled to stand them back up, while another raced ahead in an attempt to move cones before the trailer got there. It was a great show, and I laughed through it all.

The very best part was the other half of the mobile-home I could see about a quarter mile in the distance...

Illinois was making more "speed bumps" on I-55. Actually, they were repairing the road, sawing out cracked areas and filling the resulting hole with new concrete. They never seemed to get the new pour to the same level as the surrounding concrete, resulting in an annoying washboard effect as you travelled the road. At any rate, the construction crew used cones to restrict the traffic to the left lane. As they sawed-dug-replaced the concrete sections, they'd move the cones further along the highway. Day by day, the whole construction zone would migrate down the Interstate.

It was barely dawn, and I couldn't see another vehicle anywhere on the road as I entered the construction zone on a Saturday morning. Then, I got a little carless and wandered too far to the right. That's when I accidentally discovered that if I hit a cone *just right*; just a *kiss* with the side of the trailer tire, I could send it skittering all the way off the side of the road like an errant bowling pin. It was something that needed further investigation. After all, I wouldn't be actually *harming* the cones, just sort of relocating them to another spot.

I experimented a little, hitting a few, missing a few. I figured out that the trick was to steer towards a cone, and then left, away from it; missing it with the steer tire up front but leaving the orange plaything directly in the path of the trailer tires. I learned that the cones were spaced too closely together to get every one, but I if I maneuvered correctly, I could get every *other* one. I devised a scoring system, giving myself one point for every one I knocked all the way off the road. I gave myself zero points for a miss, of course, and I even deducted points if I ran the cone over. Only a skitter off the side of the road would count in my newly-invented sport.

By the time I got to the end of the construction zone, I had gotten *good*. I missed a few, at first, and I crushed a few, but before long I had no trouble convincing myself that I was some sort of cone-skittering champion. I could remove every-other cone, often racking up six or eight without a miss. I kept an eye out for state troopers, since they might not have the same sense of humor as I did about the little orange critters. But, my skill kept improving, and I got to where I could knock them flying almost at will. I think my best was twenty-two or something like it. The championship was mine!

I was almost sorry to see the construction zone end, which is a pretty rare sensation for a truck driver. But, end it did, and I moved back into the right lane, still skittering cones as the orange line veered off to the right. That's when I finally saw the car that had been close on my tail all the way through the zone. Thankfully, it wasn't the dreaded state trooper I initially feared.

It was just four highly-appreciative younger guys, laughing and waving as they passed by on a sunny Saturday morning.

A few days later, I demonstrated my new-found skill to another driver. Working for the same company, we were running together with him about a quarter-mile behind my trailer. Once he noticed what I was doing, he decided that he'd give it a try, too. I gave him a little CB radio advice, but not much. I knew that state troopers have CB radios, too. I could see him get a few, but it was necessary to concentrate on my own efforts. From what I had seen, I had no doubt that my championship was intact. What could it hurt to pass my new-found skill to another driver?

About twenty minutes down the road from the construction zone, he was pulled over by the Illinois State Patrol. As he steered to the shoulder, he told me on the CB that he'd catch up to me later, when he arrived at our delivery point. I wished him luck and went on my way.

Of course, when we met up I asked him why he was stopped and if he had received a ticket. He had indeed, for "mischievous conduct." The officer had said was for abusing the orange traffic cones. "How did he know it was you?" I asked. "I tried to deny it," he said, "but the officer made me get out of the truck and then he showed me an orange cone that got trapped under my steering axle. I guess I had been dragging it down the highway ever since the construction zone. I didn't have an excuse. So, I got the ticket."

I really felt bad for him, and I told him so.

On the other hand, I *was* still the champion…

Chapter 19 - The Guard

Any driver who has picked up or delivered more than a handful of loads has encountered a security guard. Just like drivers, most are honest folks just trying to make a living. But there are a few that have been known to take their position of authority just a little too seriously...

I received the news from my dispatcher with mixed emotions. Winter storms had played havoc with the nation's rail system, causing massive delivery delays. Due to failed deliveries, the foundry in Ironton, Ohio needed emergency loads of casting sand and was willing to pay a premium price for them. While I was glad to get the load, I would need to push hard to make the delivery appointment time. I had been looking forward to a shower and a good meal, but those plans would have to wait.

As I waited in the loading line, I began to doubt that I would make delivery on time. Then there was a problem with the fuel card at the truck stop, and some road construction too. Despite the delays, I pushed on without a break and was only ten minutes late when I pulled into the foundry in Ironton. A uniformed guard that couldn't have weighed more than one-ten sauntered out to meet me, clipboard in hand.

"You're late," he said, after reviewing my paperwork. I started to explain the late dispatch and the other issues I had dealt with, but he would have none of it. "The reason we make appointments," he said, "is to get you truckers through here efficiently. When you're late, it delays the whole process." I tried to interrupt, but he jabbed his finger at my chest for emphasis; "You need to plan your trips so you'll have time to get here on time." He rose up to all of his 5-foot, 2-inch frame. "I have a mind to make you park it until everyone else on the schedule is unloaded. That will be tomorrow morning!"

I was not in a mood to let this Barney Fife lookalike chew me out after the effort I had made to get there. Images of the old Andy Griffith show came to mind, and I half expected the guard to start rummaging through his pockets for the one bullet he was allowed to carry.

Still, the prospect of spending 24 hours waiting to unload was not a pretty one. I swallowed hard and told him how sorry I was for being late. I promised that I would do better next time. "I'll let it go this time," Barney grunted. "But you'd better be on time in the future." He made me wait for an hour or so to make sure I got the point, and then let me pull up to be unloaded.

Funny thing about those winter storms; they tend to happen all winter long. It was only a few weeks later that the railroad failed again and, once again, I was dispatched on an emergency load to Ironton. The trip went without a hitch, and I pulled into the foundry gate early. Barney was there again, this time with bad news.

"The conveyor system is down," he said, matter-of-factly. "No one gets unloaded until we get it fixed. Park it over there," he pointed, "and I'll call you on the CB radio when it's your turn." I asked if he had an idea how long that would be. "How should I know?" he snapped. "Just park it over there..."

The image of the diminutive guard jabbing his finger into my chest and chewing my tail on my last visit flashed through my mind, and I decided that Barney needed a new attitude. "The reason we make appointments," I said, jabbing my finger into his skinny, uniformed chest, "is to get these trucks through here efficiently! When you fail to maintain your conveyor system, it delays the whole process!"

The shocked look on his face said it all. "I'm sorry," he said, "but sometimes things happen that we can't control." "Really?" I asked, towering over him. At my short height, there aren't many men I can "tower" over, and I took full advantage. "You mean, like road construction, or weather, or loading delays; you know, the things that can make a truck driver late even when he's busted his butt to get here?" Recognition flashed in his eyes as I continued. "Maybe you feel you don't deserve the blame when things like this go wrong?" He nodded. "Well, neither did I when I got here late a couple of weeks ago and you chewed me out like a tardy school kid."

Barney looked as if he was about to cry. "What do you want me to do?" he said. "Sign here," I said, pulling out the load manifest. I wrote "Detention charges $75 per hour" and the current time. He signed without comment. "One more thing," I said. "I'll be sleeping while I wait, so don't be planning to call me on the CB radio. You walk over and knock on the door when it's my turn. Got it?" He did.

$675 later, Barney tapped on the door to wake me from the best night of sleep ever.

Chapter 20 - More Fishin'

This doesn't have anything to do with trucking, but my brother and I wanted to take our father fishing. He's getting on in years and may not be able to get around to enjoy it much longer. We booked a trip to one of those fly-in "wilderness" lodges in Canada, and I parked the truck for some well-deserved recreation time.

From the window of the float-plane that brought us to the place, we could see the logging road that ran right up to the back side of the lodge. I guess it wasn't quite as "wilderness" as we had thought, but to us it was still wonderful. The scenery was magnificent and we caught a ton of fish. Walleyes, Northern Pike, Smallmouth Bass: we were having a great time. Back at the lodge, they fed us like a crew of hungry lumberjacks; we couldn't have been happier.

I had discovered early that the smallmouth bass loved the little red spinner baits I had stocked in my tackle box. Unfortunately, so did underwater trees and rocks that snagged them, and I was soon down to my last one. There was no bait and tackle store close by where I could replenish my supply. After all, we had flown in to the lodge.

I found a can of red spray paint in the boat shed, which matched the color of the stripe painted on each boat that belonged to the lodge. I used it to "customize" a few lures of other, less effective colors. But, it wasn't long before I lost those, too, and was once again down to one. I determined to make every effort to protect my last little red spinner.

Early one morning, I walked from our cabin down to the dock to wait for with Dad and brother, who had not yet finished breakfast. I placed my tackle box in one of the boats that were moored there, and picked up a fishing rod for a few casts from the dock while I waited.

About thirty feet of water separated the dock from a vertical, granite wall about fifty feet high. I thought there may be some smallies lurking around the base of that big rock, and I was right. I caught several, releasing them into the cold Canadian lake. Then, I saw a small bush, right at the water's edge, clinging tenaciously to a crack in the granite. I just knew there would be a giant smallmouth hiding beneath that bush, and I carefully cast my last little red spinner bait towards it. It landed right in the heart of the bush.

It wouldn't budge. I could see it, right at the end of a branch. I pulled, relaxed, moved side-to-side; the little bush was securely hooked to my last spinner bait. With a sigh, I decided further action was needed if I was to save the lure. I untied one of the boats at the dock, reasoning that it wouldn't take more than three or four strokes of the paddle to get over to the offending bush and retrieve my spinner bait. I positioned myself in the bow of the boat, kneeling to lean out as far as possible. I paddled, and then lay the paddle down to reach out for the lure.

My intent was to take hold of the branch and pull the boat close enough to untangle the bait from the offending branch. My hand came within an inch of the lure, and all forward momentum stopped. In fact, it seemed that a light current was gently drifting the boat *away* from the little bush. I picked up the paddle and gave a couple of strokes. Once again, the boat stopped with the lure just out of my reach and began to drift away.

I'm not sure what words I muttered, but I was determined to retrieve my lure. I paddled furiously, aiming directly at the bush. I pictured the boat bouncing off the rocks with a loud bang, but I didn't care; I wasn't giving up on that spinner. To my chagrin, the boat once again stopped within a fraction of an inch of my target. I'm sure that my words were, to say the least, "colorful," but I gave it another try. This time I was going to make it. I paddled hard and leaned precariously over the bow of the boat, a foot away. Six inches. Three. One inch. Just a little more…

And then I heard the voice of my little brother. Unbeknownst to me, he had picked up the other end of the line tied to the back end of the boat I used. The end that used to be tied to the dock.

"Did you want me to let go of this rope?" he asked. He had been pulling it back ever-so-gently each time I got close to the lure, struggling to hold back his laughter. Then I heard my father laughing, along with several other guests of the lodge who had left their breakfast on the table and stepped outside to witness the show that Brother and I were putting on at the dock.

Politely, I asked if he would please let go of the rope so I could retrieve my lure, which I did.

Oh, I got him back. But, that's another fishin' story.

Chapter 21 - Stupid

There was plenty of warning. The orange signs warned of construction five miles in advance, and repeated their "Right Lane Closed" message every mile. Two miles from the construction zone, flashing signs augmented the orange ones. After that, signs were spaced at half-mile increments; then at 1,000-foot increments. It doesn't seem possible that anyone on the road did not know the right lane was ending.

At two miles out, I turned on my left turn signal and started looking for room to make a lane change. Traffic was super heavy and the left lane was already crowded. Finding room for a tractor trailer was not going to be easy. Car after car passed as the distance between my truck and the closed right lane steadily shrank. One mile. One-half mile. 2,000 feet. Finally, I saw a space in the distance that might be big enough. Right after that red car passes, and if that white one doesn't speed up to close the gap.

Ahead, I saw the barrels that closed the lane. They started on the right shoulder, each one strategically placed just a few inches closer to the center line to force traffic to the left. Checking the mirror again, I saw that the space I had seen earlier was almost upon me. I would have preferred a larger space, but it was either change lanes now, or hit the brakes to avoid the barrels ahead. Besides, my turn signal had been on for nearly two miles. Surely, that white car was expecting me to move into the lane. As soon as the red car passed, I checked my space one last time and began the lane change. I checked the white car one more time and saw that I had room, but it was closer than I would have liked. I kept moving to the left and then noticed something odd; the nose of the white car had risen, and I knew what that meant.

The driver was accelerating; deliberately trying to fill the space ahead before I could move into it. I was already moving left, with nowhere else to go. Committed to the lane change, I removed any temptation for the driver of the white car to pass by rapidly completing the maneuver, occupying the lane. "Stupid," I thought, settling in for a long construction zone. Then I saw something that shocked me. The white car was in the median. In the grass. "Surely I hadn't forced him out of the road," I thought. There wasn't as much room as I would have liked, but there *was* enough. And, I was right. I hadn't forced the vehicle off the road.

He was passing. In the median, driving on grass, through a construction zone with traffic moving at fifty miles-per-hour, he was attempting to pass my truck.

I did nothing, hoping he would come to his senses. If I slowed to allow him to pass, traffic behind me would close up and he would not have a space to move into if he changed his mind. If I accelerated to keep him from passing, I would lose the safe following distance between my truck and the red car ahead, and he'd have nowhere to go if he completed the maneuver. I could only hope that he would smarten-up and start driving like he had some sense. But he continued to gain ground moving up alongside my trailer.

Up ahead, I could see more road construction signs, placed in the median and anchored there with sandbags piled across their steel legs. As his car came up even with the door of my truck, I realized he could not complete the pass before hitting the next sign. I took my foot off the throttle, preparing to make room for him before he crashed. I looked down to see if he was taking advantage of the space I was giving.

I looked directly into a set of huge, terrified brown eyes. It was a woman, probably his wife, in the passenger seat looking right up at me. I saw the baby, too, safely strapped into the child seat in back, right behind the mother. Then the white car suddenly slowed, veering into the space immediately behind my trailer. And I started shaking.

It was about as angry as I have ever been behind the wheel of a truck. This person, this idiot, had just risked the lives of his wife and baby daughter, along with his own, for what? To prove to the big, bad truck driver that he belonged in front? Traffic was bumper-to-bumper in the only open lane, so what difference did it make where his car fit in the traffic column?

Maybe he felt I had cut him off and he was trying to make a point. Killing his family just didn't seem like the way to do it.

As soon as we came out of the construction zone and two lanes were again available, I moved to the right and the white car passed. I kept my eyes straight ahead, trying to avoid eye contact that might lead to a confrontation. I was prepared if he tried to cut back in front to exact his revenge. He had already demonstrated that he was capable of such stupidity. But, he continued ahead, staying in the left lane.

Blue signs informed us of a Rest Area up ahead, and I decided to take a short break to calm down. My plans changed when I saw the white car move from the left lane across to the exit ramp on the right. I wanted to follow; to tell the guy exactly what I thought of his stupidity. No, I really wanted to take him by the shirt collar and bang his head off of his car a time or three to make sure he got the point.

I decided it probably wouldn't be a good idea to follow his stupid decision with one of my own.

Still shaking, I went my way. Even today, I can still see those eyes...

Chapter 22 - Stupider

I was really tired. The foundry was working overtime, ordering back-to-back loads of sand, used to make the molds in which engine parts were cast. I was making the triangle; Bridgman, Michigan, to Peoria, Illinois to Ottawa, Illinois and back to Bridgman. I was pushing hard to take advantage of the opportunity to make extra money. I'd just finished two consecutive rounds, usually two days work. I'd been going for over 30 hours solid, stopping only for fuel and coffee or to load or unload. It wasn't smart, but it paid well and I needed the money. I parked the truck and called Charles, the dispatcher to tell him I was going to bed.

"I need your help," Charles told me. "The driver Tom hired to drive his truck? Well, he rolled it over up in Michigan and he has no way to get home. Could you bring him back with you?" "Wish I could help," I said, "but I can't go any further. I need some sleep." "Sleep?" was his reply. "That's what weekends are for!"

I argued with him and I should have just hung up the phone, but I didn't. The clincher was when he said, "Look, you can be there in a couple of hours. He's been sitting around all day so he's rested. You can climb in the bunk and he can drive for you." What a plan, I thought. "Didn't you just tell me he needs a ride because he rolled a truck over?" I asked, incredulous. "I really appreciate this, and I know Tom does too," he replied.

In those days when log books were frequently abused, we had a system at that company that we used whenever a driver had exceeded legal driving hours. We would complete the log on the trip just as we had done it, but would not sign or date the log. Every mechanic in the company's shop had a Commercial Driver's License. I'd tear the log page out, and one of those mechanics would sign it just as if *he* had done the driving that day. Then, I'd make out another log page, showing myself off-duty for the whole day. It wasn't legal, but as long as everybody kept making money and the police didn't find out, it worked. I'm not proud of it, but that's how things were often done in those days.

I loaded up in Ottawa and then loaded up with coffee before merging back into Interstate traffic. The sun was still bright and I felt like I could make it, but I knew it would get worse once the sun went down. It did. I arrived in Bridgman just after dark. Since I unloaded and reloaded at the same facility, it didn't take long before I was ready to head for Peoria with my new passenger. Tom had hired him only a week earlier and he didn't impress me when he climbed into the tractor and said, "Boy, am I *tired*!" "I understand," I told him. "Wrecking trucks will wear you out pretty fast." I explained to him that I had been up for more than 36 hours myself, and suggested that if he didn't want to experience a second truck rollover he'd better keep both coffee and conversation flowing.

I don't remember the rest of the trip to Peoria, or the leg back to Ottawa. There weren't any scratches or dents on the front of the truck, so I assumed I hadn't hit anything. But, the hours spent making that trip were gone from my memory, as was any recollection of my passenger. To this day, I cannot tell you what he looked like or what he wore or if he was tall or skinny or whatever. All I knew was that Ottawa was an hour from my home and I'd soon be asleep in my own bed. As soon as I dropped off my passenger, I called my wife to tell her and I warned her not to get between me and the bed when I came through the door. Then, I headed north on I-39.

A half-hour later I pulled into a truck stop and called her again. "I have nodded off three times that I know of," I said. "I don't think it would be a good idea to drive the rest of the way. In fact, I'm *afraid* to drive the rest of the way. I'll sleep here." She was very understanding, of course. My alarm clock said it was 2:00 when I heaved myself onto the mattress, but I didn't set a wake up time.

I woke up a little past 7:00, according to my trusty clock. I was still sleepy, but I knew that the restaurant closed at nine and there would be no dinner for me if I didn't get dressed and go inside. Reasoning that I could go back to sleep after eating, I pulled on my clothes and climbed down from the tractor. There was still plenty of light since it was summer and dusk didn't arrive until nearly 9:00.

I sat down at a table and a cheery waitress brought a menu. "They must have 24-hour a day breakfast," I thought, searching the menu for a hamburger and finding only eggs and pancakes. "I'll just have the buffet," I told the waitress. "Help yourself," she said, pointing to a tall stack of plates. But I was as confused at the buffet cart as I had been when reading the menu. It was full of food all right; scrambled eggs and sausage and bacon and French toast and biscuits and hash-brown potatoes and fruit.

The waitress went by and I waved her down and asked what a guy had to do to get a hamburger. "The cook doesn't start on lunch until ten-thirty," she said. My befuddled brain slowly began to figure it out. To be sure, I stepped over to the newspaper box by the front door and discovered that the paper on display had tomorrow's date printed on it. No, *today's* date. I had slept for seventeen hours; from 2:00 p.m. right through to the next morning. The pancakes were good, I think.

It is necessary that I put this account in perspective. It was, by far, the stupidest thing I ever did as a driver. I realize how incredibly fortunate I was not to have hurt someone, or myself, while driving in this fatigued condition. I never did it again.

Please don't ever do that.

Chapter 23 - Songs

Even truckers have hobbies, right? I've been known to catch a fish or two, and I've planted my share of tomatoes and cucumbers in my day, but those activities are difficult to pursue on the road. But, I can sing anytime. In fact, the way I sing, it's probably better that I do it when I'm on the road, *alone*.

I learned a long time ago that I'm pretty good at writing, and I like doing it. I've written poems, stories, songs, letters, you name it. I wrote most of the driver manual still used by one trucking company. I wrote much of their safety program, too. Letters to the editor, newsletter articles, photo captions. Like I said, I like to write.

My dream, of course, is to make millions from my music and live happily ever after. But, I keep my CDL current, just in case it doesn't happen.

Of more than a hundred songs I've written or co-written, ten are drawn from my trucking experience. I couldn't have written them if I hadn't spent time on the road, living the trucking life. As of this date, my most well-known song is "Lines on the Highway," recorded by Larry Sparks on his "Almost Home" album, released in March, 2011. I co-wrote that song with my friend "Big" Al Weekley, who is a disc jockey for KRVN radio out of Lexington, Nebraska. If you're a Bluegrass fan, you know that Sparks is an icon of the genre. If you're not a Bluegrass fan, you're missing out on some great music.

The chorus of the song goes like this:
Those lines on the highway take me where I want to go
Yeah, those lines on the highway,
they take me where I want to go
There's diesel in my bloodlines,
and highway lines are painted on my soul
© 2006, Cliff Abbott, Jr.

I co-wrote two others with Big Al, including the duet
"Victim of a Truck Driver's Life:"
There's kids to feed and bills to pay
And we're apart another day
Victims of a truck driver's life
©2004 Cliff Abbott, Jr.

There's also this one, "Reflections of My Life," from Big Al
and me:
Success can take a lifetime when you build it load by load
Many times I have wondered, should I take a different road?
Reflections in the windshield; the face I see is mine
It paints a worried picture, Reflections of my Life

I wrote a song called Sandstone, about the wreck I had when
I lost my brakes on that mountain in West Virginia. That story
is the subject of the first chapter of this book. The song's
closing line is good advice for any truck driver:

Don't take the mountain lightly or it might be your last ride.
© 2003, Cliff Abbott, Jr.
For me, it nearly was.

Being a romantic sort, I wrote a song for my wife, too. Like
many drivers, I didn't know what to say when I left for the road.

Goodbye? Well, it wasn't goodbye; I was just going to work. Still, I wouldn't be home that night, or the next, or the one after. I thought a lot about what she'd want me to say and finally came up with this:

I'll be coming home to you, Sweetheart,
with the breaking of the dawn
With the falling of the dew, you'll know
you're my only special one
When we've said our last goodbye and death
takes us from the world we knew
If there's Heaven in the sky, Sweetheart,
I'll be coming home to you
© 1991 Cliff Abbott, Jr.

There's one called, "Highway State of Mind" that says:

There's a concrete river flowing in the distance to the West
And, the humming of the highway is the song I like the best
The life I love is here between the lines,
They keep me in a highway state of mind
©2007 Cliff Abbott, Jr.

My faith is reflected in "Truck Driver's Prayer," with:

Put your hand on my shoulder, Jesus,
guide me through this day.
©2003 Cliff Abbott, Jr.

Then there's my ballad about that super-trucker we all know, whose name is in the Chorus:

I'm Billy Big Rigger, and everywhere I go
I ain't just driving a truck, Lord,
I'm putting on a show
I'm Billy Big Rigger, as you can plainly see
I'll bet you wish you could be,
Billy Big Rigger like me
©2002 Cliff Abbott, Jr.

I've got another one about a guy who calls home and can't wait to be there with his baby:

Now I'm flying down the mountain
and sliding 'round the curve
I'd like to leave them brakes alone,
but I ain't got the nerve
I left my coffee sitting on the table by the phone
My baby said she loves me,
got these big wheels rollin' home
©2003 Cliff Abbott, Jr.

I suppose my lawyer would advise me to tell you that I don't recommend actually "flying down the mountain and sliding 'round the curve." Or maybe that the song is about "a professional driver on a closed course. Do not attempt." Your mileage may vary, of course.

If there's one song among those I have written that best exemplifies my feelings about professional drivers, it is spelled out in the song, "American Trucker." Much of the song details the many, many things that truckers bring to America. The song begins:

Who brought the food on your table?
Who brought the gas in your car?

The song brings it home in the chorus, with these words:
Hello, American Trucker
You got American soul
Ride on, American Trucker
You're the rock that makes America Roll!
©2002 Cliff Abbott, Jr.

I maintain a website at www.cliffsongs.com for anyone who wants to hear segments of some of these songs. Maybe someday I'll put them all on one CD and try to market it. But, unless I win the lottery, I need to sell some books, first!

Of course my dream is that someday trucking music will be huge again, as it was in the days of Dave Dudley, Red Sovine, and other Country Music heroes. I'm from the generation that still remembers great trucking songs like, "Giddyup Go" and "Six Days on the Road." If you're a fan of the movie, "Smoky and the Bandit," you probably remember the Jerry Reed hit, "Eastbound and Down." I'm probably being nostalgic, but I miss music like that. I know that my writing was influenced by it.

I have resigned myself to the reality that I probably won't get rich from my music. I can always dream that someday far in the future some driver who was born long after I'm gone will be going down some galactic highway, jamming to

"There's diesel in my bloodline, and highway lines are painted on my soul…"

Chapter 24 - Chicken Gizzards

Every driver who has spent time on the road has accumulated stories about various dealings with law enforcement officials. In other chapters, I have discussed one or two encounters that did not go so well for me. This is one that turned out OK.

My favorite part of the chicken is the gizzard. Some people think that's kind of nasty, but if you had a Momma like mine who can cut up and fry a chicken good enough to make a Colonel cry, you'd understand. We never considered ourselves poor, but in the home I grew up in, we wasted nothing. When Momma fried a chicken, she fried it all, including the neck, liver, heart; all those things that come stuffed inside that people usually call "giblets." The gizzard belonged to Daddy; that's just how it was. We could have any other piece, and Daddy would take what was left, but the gizzard was his.

My brother and I settled for drumsticks, but we knew that someday we would grow up and head our own households. Then, we would be entitled to the gizzard any time the families we headed had fried chicken. It was a rite of passage. I was surprised to learn that it wasn't the same in *every* family.

As you may be aware, fried chicken gizzards are not readily available at most truck stops. Even places with fast-food restaurants specializing in chicken don't serve gizzards, although I saw chicken livers on the menu at one place. Not everyone appreciates a good gizzard like I do, I suppose. At any rate, I stopped at a truck stop in Columbia, South Carolina once; I think it was called the "All American Truck Stop." I don't know if it's still there; it's been a long time. As I recall, it wasn't fancy, but it was long past lunch time and it would do for fuel and a quick meal. I glanced over the menu board while I waited in line, trying to decide if I'd get the three or the four-piece meal. And then I saw it; *fried gizzards*. There was no two-piece this or three-piece that; you got the half-pound box of gizzards or you got the whole pound box of gizzards. I was in love...

The elderly black lady behind the counter gave me a knowing smile when I placed my order. "How many biscuits do you want with your gizzards, *hon*?" She asked, holding up the cardboard box that would soon hold my delightful dinner. "No room for a biscuit," I told her. "Just put all the gizzards you can fit in that box, and a Diet Coke™." Don't try to figure out the Diet Coke thing; I can't explain it. Yeah, I'm one of those guys who has a Diet Coke with my candy bar. Just accept it.

It was all I could do not to open the gizzards until the city traffic was behind me. There they sat, on the doghouse of my cabover Freightliner, filling the cab with their tantalizing aroma.

For the non-trucking reader, the "doghouse" is the engine cover, or "hump" between the driver and passenger seats in a cabover truck. And, a "cabover" is a truck with no nose, or no hood with the engine underneath. The truck's cab sits "over" the engine, hence "cabover." But, let's get back to chicken gizzards, shall we?

Just when I was about to dig in for the first heavenly bite of gizzard, I saw the "weigh station" sign. I decided to wait until I passed the coop, and I was dismayed to see the trooper-mobile parked on the side with an officer watching my approach, clipboard in hand. I knew this couldn't be good.

Oh, he was a nice guy. He told me that I was, unfortunately, destined to be the unlucky recipient of one of the three inspections he would perform today. He placed my Commercial Driver's License under the clip on his clipboard and wrote down the information printed on it. Then, he did something no other uniformed officer has ever asked me to do; he asked that I accompany him on his walk around the tractor and trailer, so that we could discuss any deficiencies he found right on the spot. And, that's what we did. He'd say, "I'm looking for a fluid leak *here*," and "I'm looking for chafing, *here*;" each time pointing to the truck part he was inspecting before making another mark on his clipboard. I'd say "Uh-huh," and nod my head in agreement. You just can't be too careful about leaking and chafing, you know.

We ended our little stroll where we started; in front of his cruiser. He leaned against the car's grill and told me that the vehicle portion of the inspection was over. Then, he asked me to retrieve my paperwork from the cab so we could finish up the driver portion.

My face must have betrayed my emotion. "What's wrong?" he asked, pointing out that he had found no deficiencies at all on the tractor or trailer. "You do have a logbook and a load manifest, don't you?" he asked. "Of course," I told him. "Then, what's the problem?" he asked. "No problem," I told him. "It's just that…," and I told him about the now nearly-cold box of fried chicken gizzards still sitting on the engine cover in my tractor.

"Is your logbook up to date?" he asked? "Yes, Sir," I told him. "Got your load manifest and your medical card; all in good order?" he queried. "Yes, Sir," I said, "I'll get them for you." "Don't worry about it," he replied. "Enjoy your gizzards. And, drive safely."

I could have kissed him...

Chapter 25 - Old Town Scale

It didn't look much bigger than a phone booth, that scale house in Old Town. It sat right in the middle of US Highway 90, with traffic lanes on either side. I'd never seen it open, although I'd been through the Florida town numerous times. I didn't give it a second thought as I approached just after midnight, but I should have.

I was nearing the end of a bad week. Breakdowns and delays had cost a lot of time and I had run hard to make up for it. I was long overdue for some sleep. Plus, I hadn't showered or shaved for several days, and I knew I looked raggedy. I hadn't touched my log book, either, planning to catch it all up when I arrived at my delivery point in the morning. It's not the way I usually did things, but, as I said, it was a bad week.

I saw the lights from a distance, but my mind refused to believe the scale was open until the officer waved me on to the weighing platform. I hoped they would see that the weight was OK and wave me on, but it wasn't to be. A state trooper popped out of the door to the office and walked directly to my door. He was pleasant enough, greeting me warmly when I cranked down the window. He even asked if I was enjoying the warm gulf weather. He looked at my CDL, handed it back, and then asked for my Record of Duty Status. And, I laughed.

I'm still not sure what I found so humorous. Maybe it was the irony of the tiny scale house being open one time out of the dozen I had been through there. Maybe it was the fact that my log book was checked on the very rare occasion that it was several days behind. Maybe I was so worn out that I just didn't respond appropriately. Nonetheless, I couldn't withdraw my giggles and I knew it. "What's so funny?" the bemused officer asked. "See for yourself," I told him as I handed my log book out of the open window.

It seemed to take a great deal of time as the officer flipped page after page. "This looks good," he said, "except for the last three days." "I know," I told him. "It's been a hell of a week."

I waited, nervously, as he obviously considered how many citations to write. Finally, he looked up from his study. "See that wide spot, right up there?" he asked, pointing to a parking area just ahead. "Yes, Sir," I told him, fearing the worst. "I would suggest," he said, "that you pull up there and get this log book up to date, before *somebody* gives you a ticket!"

It wasn't easy, and I'll admit that some of my entries were somewhat "creative," but I brought the duty record up to the minute and neat as a pin. When done, I gathered up log book, load papers, and even the permit book and walked back to the scale house.

There were several officers inside, and they all looked up when I entered. I quickly identified the one who I had dealt with earlier. "I'm finished with my log book," I announced. "Is it up to date?" he responded. "Yes, Sir," I replied. "Would you like to inspect it?" "Nope," he said. Have a nice night, Driver. Get some rest."

A few miles further, I found a place to park and took the nice officer's advice.

Chapter 26 - Liars

I can't tell you how many times I've heard a driver claim he was lied to by a recruiter or a dispatcher. As a driver, I was first recruited by a school and then by a number of companies, all of which had dispatchers to direct my work. Years later, I taught at a CDL school and I have managed recruiters and dispatchers. I've been on both sides of the equation. I have been promised utopia-on-wheels by certain recruiters. I have also fired recruiters for being less than honest, so I know that it happens. I also know that there are certain drivers who always seem to hear something other than what they are told. Here are some examples I have witnessed:

Recruiter says: "We replace our trucks regularly. We have new ones coming in all the time!"
Driver hears: "You'll get a brand-new truck!"

Recruiter says: "Our top team averaged 6,200 miles per week last quarter."
Driver hears: "We have a 6,200 mile-per-week guarantee!"

Recruiter says: "Our Southeast Regional Fleet runs mostly Georgia, Alabama, and the Carolinas."
Driver hears: "I promise, we'll never send you to Tennessee, where your ex-wife has a warrant out for you."

I'm not saying you will never be lied to. I'm saying, stuff happens. Listen carefully and ask for clarification if you aren't sure of what you heard. Remember that the person on the other end of the conversation is a person, too. Give them the benefit of the doubt, as you expect them to do for you. And ask yourself; if you're convinced that they're really lying to you, do you really want to be working for them anyway?

As a Recruiting Manager, I did not tolerate dishonesty from recruiters *or* drivers. As stated earlier, I have fired recruiters who I found to be less than truthful with applicants. On the other hand, I simply didn't hire drivers who falsified their employment applications. You'd be amazed how many times the driver recorded zero traffic convictions on the application when, in fact, he had three or four. "Oh, *those* tickets!" they'd say, when the report came back. "I forgot about those." Oops.

My favorites were the ones that spent 8 years in the penitentiary and stated on the application that they had never been convicted of a crime. Their record would show up in the reports and I'd call them. "Well, they *said* I held up a liquor store," I'd hear. "But I was waiting in the car while my buddy got some cigarettes. I didn't have any idea he was robbing the place!" I'd tell these geniuses the same thing: "The judge and jury had a lot more evidence to see than I did, and they didn't believe you. What makes you think I will?"

In the employment section of the job application, one creative applicant listed that he had worked for seven years at the Texas Department of Corrections as a "Pastry Chef." We called the phone number he provided, but the person we spoke with could not find any record of his employment. She assured us that the Texas Department of Corrections hired many people, including kitchen help. However, she simply couldn't find a record of this guy's employment. After many minutes on the phone, she announced that she was going to conference in another department. We could hear the phone ringing and then a pleasant voice answered, "Inmate Records..." To be accurate, I guess I'd have to admit that the driver didn't really lie. He had, indeed, worked in the kitchen of the Texas Department of Corrections. I guess they fired him when his sentence was up.

Dispatchers get a bad rap for their honesty, too. Like recruiters, sometimes the reputation is deserved and sometimes the driver hears what he or she wants to. Like this:

Dispatcher says: "A driver has had a death in the family and I'm assigning your load to him so he can get home. I'll get with the load planner and find you another load as quickly as I can."
Driver hears: "I'm taking your load away to punish you for that load you refused last week. Take that, you lug nut!"

Dispatcher says: "I'm sorry, but the customer cancelled your load. I'm working on another one for you."
Driver hears: "See that truck going out the gate? I gave him *your* load because I like him better. *You* suck!"

Sometimes a lie is deliberate, too. Like the time a driver I knew claimed he needed to be home one weekend for his grandmother's funeral. I guess he didn't realize his dispatcher was counting. It was the seventh grandmother he buried, poor guy. Family first, I guess.

What do *you* say when the police officer asks how fast you were going? "Uh, I was going forty-eight, officer, and the speed limit is thirty five. Go ahead, write me a ticket. I deserve it." Right? Of course, I never told a lie when I was driving. If you don't believe me, you can check my log book...

I'll end the chapter with this incident: When I hauled petroleum, I was dispatched on five loads of diesel fuel to a

Georgia truck stop. It was an easy day, just a shuttle between loading facility and truck stop, five times. The weather reports were calling for snow flurries and, sure enough, a few flakes were in the air. Very few. In fact, it wasn't even a dusting. After my second load, I picked up a pay phone to check in with the office. As I dialed, I heard the driver next to me yelling into his phone. "I'm telling you, I'm shutting *down!*" he said. "The roads are *impassible!*" he continued. "I'm *not* gonna have an accident for your stupid load!" I laughed as I walked back to the truck, and didn't even slow down as I delivered the next three loads on perfectly dry roads.

Chapter 27 - CSA

This chapter will primarily take the form of a rant. It won't be funny. In fact, I hope you're as mad as I am after you read it. In an attempt to share safety information so that companies can make more informed decisions about which drivers to hire, our government created CSA, which stands for Compliance, Safety, Accountability. In my opinion, it represents nothing less than the betrayal of the American truck driver. Although the intent is to make the roads safer for everyone, CSA violates our basic civil rights as Americans, and the sooner some court throws it out, the better.

Someone, soon, will file the lawsuit that makes it happen, if it hasn't been filed already.

Let me preface my comments with a hypothetical situation. Suppose you received a letter from your credit card company that looks like this:

Dear Customer,

Our records indicate that your payment, due on the first of the month, was not received by this office. Because your payment was not received, we are cancelling your credit card, and we are increasing interest rate on your remaining balance to 25%. Additionally, we will report the failed payment to credit reporting agencies, so that it will appear on your credit record. Have a nice day...

Sincerely,

Your EX Credit Card Company

You're pretty sure you made that credit card payment, so you check your records. Sure enough, you *did* mail the payment, and on time, too. Your bank even has a copy of the cancelled check. So, you call the credit card folks, and they agree. Their records were in error. They received the payment. Your account will be credited immediately. They're sorry for the inconvenience, etc. Your account is in good standing, and your good credit rating is unblemished... or so you think.

Months later, you decide that it's time to trade in that junky old pickup truck on a new one. You find just the right truck and make a great deal. All that remains is the paperwork. You're waiting in the finance office, ready to trade your signature for a set of keys. But, the finance manager comes back with the bad news; the finance company has declined your loan. Of course, you ask why, and you are told that there is a missed payment showing on your credit report. "Can't be," you tell them, and you ask which credit reporting agency is reporting the missed payment.

That's when you find out that the report didn't come from a credit reporting agency. It came from *your government*. That's right; as a part of new lending regulations, the government has developed a report that banks use in considering your loan application. It's called the PLS, which stands for "Pre-Loan Screening." You can get a copy of this report, but you must pay ten dollars first, even though it contains information about you. And, you have the right to contest entries on the report. You get your copy, and you discover that the erroneous late payment is, in fact, listed. Of course, you contest the entry and ask them to fix it. After all, your old pickup won't make it much longer.

Here's where you discover the cold, hard truth. See, the report doesn't indicate that you actually *missed* a payment. It says that you were *accused* of missing a payment. That's true; you *were* accused, even if it was in error. They refuse to correct the report. The finance company understands, but they still can't approve your loan. As you ride home in your old pickup, you wonder how your own government could do such a thing to you. Aren't you supposed to be innocent until proven guilty? You were proven *not* guilty, and they reported it anyway!

I'm glad that's only a hypothetical situation, aren't you? Unfortunately, there's nothing hypothetical about the way our government treats your Commercial Motor Vehicle record under the CSA program. The only difference is that it won't be your loan application that will be declined. It will be your employment application.

The "Pre-Loan Screening" report is, in real life, the "Pre-employment Screening Program," or PSP, that was created as a part of the "CSA 2010" program, which became "CSA 2011" when it wasn't ready in time, and finally became just "CSA" when they gave up trying to meet a deadline for implementation. The concept behind the PSP is fairly simple; accumulate all the information from inspection and accident reports you have received in the past three years, and make it available to anyone who is thinking about hiring you to drive their truck.

When I managed a recruiting department, I always thought it was strange that government made it easy for me to find out if your trailer had a burned-out light bulb, but left me on my own to find out if you had failed a drug test or two. But, that's another issue.

Remember when you got pulled over for that roadside inspection in Georgia? The officer was really nice, and the inspection was absolutely clean; no deficiencies noted. All of your documents were in order, too. In only a few minutes the officer was telling you to drive safely and you were on your way, with a squeaky-clean inspection form to turn in to your safety department. Some companies even pay you a bonus for that clean inspection.

Here's what the officer didn't discuss with you: In Georgia, he can't pull you over just to do an inspection. As in the case in many other states, there must be a probable cause for the stop; at least a reasonable suspicion that you're doing something illegal and the reason for the stop must be noted on the inspection form he turns in. That form provides the data that is entered into the CSA system. If you're pulling a trailer that is missing a mud flap, you're breaking the law and can be stopped. But, your inspection was perfect, right?

Remember when the officer first greeted you at your door? He said something about how you might have been going "a little fast," and you should probably "watch your speed." No ticket was issued, not even a warning, just a friendly reminder. But, since you were stopped anyway, he went ahead with the inspection, right? Guess what's on your PSP report. SPEEDING. The date, time, and location are recorded, right along with your license number and company information.

Maybe you travel in Georgia a lot, and you get inspected, say, every six months or so. "Speeding" shows up on your report four times in the past two years. How many managers are going to approve *your* employment application? Now, consider that another driver, with a record identical to yours, *also* had four inspections in the past two years. This driver, however, drives a lot in a state where an officer doesn't need probable cause to pull over a truck to perform an inspection. Identical work records, but your PSP report says "speeding" four times, while his does not. That's fair, right?

It gets worse. Suppose you weren't driving; you were asleep in the sleeper berth when your team partner was pulled over. As a part of his inspection, the officer checked your CDL and medical card, too, and then you went back to bed. Despite the fact that you weren't driving, "speeding" will appear on *your* PSP report, too, since that was the original reason for the stop.

Unfortunately, it gets even worse; let's say you *were* ticketed for speeding. You knew you were innocent, so you went to court to fight the ticket, and you *won*. There is no penalty, since you were acquitted of the charge. Maybe the officer that wrote the ticket was so out of line that they fired him. Your PSP report *still* shows "speeding." Remember, the report doesn't say you were *convicted*; it correctly reports that you were *accused*. Actually, it doesn't even say that; it simply says "speeding." The reader can take it any way they want to.

The same is true of accident reports. No matter how minor; no matter if you were at fault, or even if your partner was driving while you slept, "accident" will show up on your PSP report.

As far as vehicle inspections go, infractions that used to be attributed to the carrier are now entries on the driver's record. If you are dispatched to pick up a preloaded trailer at 2:00 a.m., you might not pay much attention to that burned-out clearance light. After all, you don't have a bulb for it, and you don't have a ladder to reach it, anyway. Nobody is open at two in the morning that can fix it, and you're on a tight schedule. If you get inspected, you can count on that inoperative light to be on your PSP report.

In my view, it is unconscionable that *our own government* would allow, let alone require, the sharing of information of this type. As I write this, the unemployment rate in the U.S. is over 9%. Trucking companies are scrambling for drivers. Many are turning away freight because they can't hire enough of them. At the same time, our government implements a policy that causes them to turn away good drivers because of things that never should have been on their record in the first place.

Some companies will tell you. Others will keep it very general, telling you they had "better qualified candidates" without further explanation. Some will only use the information in the PSP if they feel that you are a "borderline" candidate, while others look at the PSP first. Some will give you the benefit of the doubt, while others will trash your application in a heartbeat. Many have developed a point system, where you are scored for each entry on your PSP. The same company that told you to go ahead with an overweight load may count it against you if the ticket shows up on your PSP.

Keep this in mind, too. The report is provided by the Federal Motor Carrier Safety Administration, the very same agency that has the power to shut down any trucking company they deem to be unsafe. Wouldn't that pretty much obligate every company to use the PSP, even if they question its fairness?

It's worse than unfair. Surely, it *must* be unconstitutional, and I hope somebody sues the pants off of them. Soon.

In the meantime, protect yourself. When your dispatcher tells you to take your truck and flat tire to the next truck stop, remember that doing so is illegal. If you get caught, your record will reflect the ticket you get, even if your company pays it. As much as I'd like to save the company the cost of a roadside service call, I won't risk it.

Likewise, the common practice of telling the driver to continue with an overweight load will soon be a thing of the past. Sure, they'll pay the ticket if you get one. But, will they hire you if it's on your record?

Order a copy of your PSP. Know what's on it. More importantly, understand what will go on it in the future. Protect your record; it may make all the difference next time you apply for a job.

Chapter 28 - The Cross and the Clover

If you're one of those folks who hates to discuss religion, you might want to skip this chapter. I hope you won't. It didn't cost you any extra. And, it might be something to think about, *before* you find yourself going down the mountain with no brakes. It's just that I have shared much of myself in these pages, and it wouldn't be right if I didn't share this very important part of my trucking and personal life.

I've leaned on God for a lot during my lifetime. I have considered myself a "Christian" since being very young, but my commitment wavered until, like many people of faith, I turned to God when I reached a low point in my life.

Late 1989 was a time when I felt the whole world was falling in on me. I was newly divorced, with full custody of three young children. My finances, along with my credit rating, were in shambles; a large contributor to the aforementioned divorce. The company I worked with had been sold and there was no doubt that my job would soon come to an end. The low point came on Christmas Eve, when the engine blew out in my old car, on the way to Grandma's house, no less. I had spent my last dollar on gifts for the kids and a tank of gas. Merry Christmas.

Yeah, I know, there are thousands of single mothers out there who have stories as bad as or worse than mine. They have my utmost respect. But I was keenly aware of my parental responsibilities and I knew I had to get it right for my kids. I needed *a lot* of help to do that. I looked to God for that help.

Not long after the holiday, I met the woman who became wife to me and mother to my children. With love, strength, and her own strong faith, Thresa assumed the duties of family matriarch. As expected, my job soon ended. She was everything we needed; mother, mentor, babysitter, and financial contributor. When I told her that truck-driving school would provide job opportunities that were not available locally, she cared for the kids while I learned to drive. She continued to anchor our family when my new career took me over the road for weeks at a time. Today, sitting a room away as I write, she continues to be my anchor.

The day we married, I found my first four-leaf clover. Smugly, I thought about how it represented a change in my "luck." Guilt washed over me as I considered how I had prayed for God's help, only to attribute the good things now happening in my life to luck. But, I couldn't help thinking; if God made everything, didn't He also make the four-leaf clover? Instead of an omen of luck, could they be a reminder of God's blessing?

That clover was laminated inside the wedding card I gave to Thresa. Every card I have given her since that day has had a four-leaf clover laminated inside to signify the blessing she has been to me. Yeah, I'm like that.

I have been abundantly blessed. God is *good*. I put His cross and clover on my truck for others to see, but mostly as a reminder for *me*. Besides, it kept the lot lizards from knocking so much. However, I need to make it clear that my faith is not predicated on blessings. My life isn't about what I *get* from

God. It's about what I *owe* him. I asked him for help raising my kids. He gave *His* son to die on the cross for my mistakes.

I don't deserve what He did for me. I can never repay Him. But I can share my story with others. I can ask you to think about your *eternal* destination. When this life's journey is over, where will you be, forever? Some think that there's nothing more when this life ends. To them I say, let's discuss it in, oh, a hundred years or so. If I'm right, I'll be in heaven. If *you're* right, we're both dust. Not much of a win for you, is it?

Most all of the religions in the world promise a form of life after death. Nearly all of them require you to do something to earn this eternal reward. My Bible says that you *can't* earn your way to heaven. No amount of praying, pilgrimage, or payment will get you there. Don't take my word for it. Don't take *anyone's* word for it. Read it for yourself.

Spend some time with the Bible. If you don't have one, there are truck stop chapels everywhere. Staffed with dedicated professionals, they'll provide one and answer your questions. A group called the Gideons has a mission to place one in every hotel room. *Take* it; they will gladly bring another. There's a lot of reading, but the book of Romans is a good place to start.

Here are just a few "don't miss" scriptures:

Romans 3:23 (NKJV)
"For all have sinned and fall short of the glory of God."

Romans 6:23 (NKJV)
"For the wages of sin is death, but the gift of God is eternal life in Christ Jesus our Lord."

Romans 5:8 (NKJV)
"But God demonstrates His own love toward us, in that while we were still sinners, Christ died for us."

Romans 10:13 (NKJV)
"For whoever calls on the name of the Lord shall be saved."

Maybe you'd rather read what Jesus actually said about it. If so, turn back a few pages in your bible.

John 11:25 (NKJV)
"I am the resurrection and the life. He who believes in me, though he may die, he shall live."

It's a gift. Just ask.

Epilogue

I hope this chapter doesn't read like a resume; it isn't. And, it isn't one of those "I've done it all" trucker brags, either. I simply want to convey that I come by my trucking experience honestly. Every word of this book is true. Well, OK, I *am* a trucker. As written in the Preface, most every word of this book is true, with a few *incidental* trucker embellishments. But, if you had a time machine, you could go back to when and where each recounted event actually happened and see it for yourself. Then, you could write your own book and tell it *your* way.

When I was discharged from the U.S. Army in 1979, I needed a job to support my young family, which included a pregnant wife and an almost-two-year-old son. My father had been driving a garbage truck for more than two decades, and was respected enough at his company that I got the job on not much more than his word alone. He's that kind of guy, and I knew it wasn't a gift. It was hard work, but as I said elsewhere, it was a solid, union job with good pay and benefits that let me support my young family at a time we really needed it.

The name of the company was Rot's Disposal, which many people found amusing in and of itself. Our unofficial slogan was, "Service guaranteed, or double your garbage back." We worked outside in all kinds of weather. Chicago winters can be brutal, but the days were few when we shut down because of weather. When we did, the decision was made based on driving conditions rather than driver comfort.

I wanted something more than my father's career on the garbage truck, and I left after six years for my first management position. I held several positions, including a stint as a terminal manager with the now-defunct Purolator Courier. When the company was sold, management jobs in the area were impossible to find, and I attended CDL driving school for training in a new field. I know that CDL schools don't have the best of reputations in our industry, but I attended back when courses were 6 weeks long and the students learned something about trucking, rather than just how to pass the CDL test.

My first over-the-road job was with a refrigerated carrier named "Trans-Star," out of Waupaca, Wisconsin. While there, I learned just how badly drivers can be treated at the customer's dock, especially at the grocery warehouses. I unloaded trucks, restacked pallets, and waited, a lot.

One particular customer on Snow Drift Road in Allentown, Pennsylvania banned me from their facility. I made my early-morning delivery appointment on time, and then I waited for over fifteen hours to get unloaded. No one seemed concerned that I had lost an entire day of work, and pay, because I couldn't take another load while I was sitting at their dock.

Finally, I'd had enough. I went inside and demanded to see a supervisor. When I was informed that he was unavailable due to a meeting (at eleven o'clock at night?), I said they'd better get him. I explained that he would want to see the mayonnaise flying all over their parking lot if they didn't get that d**n load off my truck, pronto. Would you believe they called my company to complain? When my dispatcher told me I would not be welcomed back, I asked, "Why would I *want* to go back?"

Another notable episode occurred when I was dispatched to Ohio with a load of ice cream. I was tired, but the dispatcher said that there was plenty of time built in to the dispatch. I'd have lots of time for a shower and some rest, once I picked up the load. I accepted but, when I tried to fuel up the truck, my fuel card was rejected. It had been turned off. That's what they did in the days before cell phones and satellite communications when they needed to talk to you. When you couldn't pay for the 150 gallons of diesel fuel you had just pumped, you'd *have* to call in. Then, they'd deliver the message and turn your fuel card back on.

In any event, when I called in, I was informed that the situation had become desperate; the customer needed that ice cream as quickly as I could get it there. And I did. I went without a shower, drank a gallon of coffee, and lied all over my log book to get there as quickly as I could. And when I arrived just a little after midnight, completely worn out, they wouldn't open the door for me. I spent a half-hour at several different doors, trying to get someone's attention. I could see them in there, and I was sure they could hear my pounding on the door, but nobody moved to answer. Disgusted, I finally gave up and went back to the truck to go to bed.

I had hardly laid down when I heard a knock at my door. "We'll take you now," said the person doing the knocking. "Why didn't you answer the door twenty minutes ago when I knocked?" I asked. "We were on break," was his answer. He explained, "We don't answer the door when we're on break." "What a coincidence," I said. "Now, *I'm* on break; an eight-hour rest break. Sorry, I can't move the truck when I'm on break. You can unload me in the morning, when my break is over." Unbelievably, they called in on me, too.

I spent a year at another management job before being bitten by the trucking bug again. That's when I bought the Mack, and leased on to a tanker company in Byron, IL. We hauled sand to different steel mills and foundries, and an occasional load of Ammonium Nitrate, used to make explosives. I still consider Bill Carlson, the owner, to be the most honest man I've ever met in trucking. Bill told you how it was, no B.S. Our industry needs a lot more like him. I left there only because my wife, who worked for the phone company, was transferred to Georgia, and I thought I should go too, being that she was raising my kids and all.

Georgia is where I got my first job hauling petroleum, and I loved it. I spent a year with Florida Rock and Tank, and then bought another tractor. I leased it to the now defunct Fleet Transport and spent the best years of my trucking life hauling jet fuel from Atlanta (Doraville), Georgia, to Knoxville and Nashville, TN. Unfortunately, another company won when the contract came up for bid, and I moved on.

I hauled Intermodal containers for a while. It was interesting, but I couldn't make it pay. Besides, after hauling jet fuel and explosives, a load of Chinese toasters wasn't the same.

In an attempt to start my own company, I bought a flatbed trailer and applied for my own authority. For the non-trucking reader, "authority" is "permission to run a trucking company," and is granted by the U.S. Department of Transportation. My newfound trucking empire lasted about six months, until the financial losses became too much to take. I discovered that the broker I got most of my loads from was skimming quite a bit of the rate off the top and passing the remainder on to me.

I will say that the flatbed drivers I encountered were, undoubtedly, the most friendly and helpful of any I have met during my trucking career. When I loaded my first steel coil, I had little idea how it was done. When the truck in front of me was loaded, I watched the driver carefully to see what he was doing. I guess I made him nervous, because he finally asked me what I was looking at. I explained that I had never hauled coiled steel before. Within seconds, a crowd of drivers was around my trailer; showing me how to place the coil racks, secure the coil, use edge protectors, throw tarps. It was a great experience.

Another time, I had picked up a load of lumber at a Florida sawmill. After loading, I pulled off to the side to tarp the load. My efforts must have looked amateurish to the driver parked beside me, and he stepped over to offer help. I freely admitted that I was a rookie. "Watch and learn," he said, and then he scurried over the loaded trailer and had the load neatly tarped in five minutes. "Wow," I said. "You sure get around a loaded trailer!" That's when he told me how much faster he used to be, before he lost his leg. He lifted his pants leg to display his artificial limb! I never got as good as him, even with two good legs. But, I learned a lot.

That same Florida sawmill was the source of another, unrelated story. When I went to the office for my paperwork, I noticed that the sand around the small building was carefully raked out in neat, symmetrical patterns. It had obviously taken someone a lot of work. I complimented the office clerk on the beauty of the manicured sand. "It ain't for beauty," he said. "The rattlesnakes mess up the lines when they crawl under the building. That's how we know when one is under there." He pointed to the cork board, and for the first time I noticed the rattlesnake rattles pinned there. *Dozens* of them. I walked back to the truck *really* carefully.

I jumped at the chance to teach at a local CDL school. It was great to be home every day, but I only stayed a few months. I felt strongly that the owner of the school was more concerned with collecting tuition and government grants than he was with graduating safe drivers. I told him so when I left.

A favorite memory is the student that several other instructors and I tried to get dismissed from school after several driving mishaps. The owner refused, stating he'd have to refund the tuition if he kicked him out. End of discussion. It was, that is, until the guy put his car's transmission in Drive when he thought it was in Reverse. In a hurry to get home after a school day, he stepped on the gas and wiped out about 30 feet of chain link fence, never taking his eyes from the back window. "How's that tuition money looking now?" I asked the owner.

The school was later closed when two instructors, who were licensed Georgia third-party road testers, were caught accepting bribes in exchange for passing grades. That's sad.

I hired someone to drive my tractor while I worked at the school, and when he quit I sold the last truck that I owned. I spent eight years at Roehl Transport, Inc., beginning as an orientation instructor in Carnesville, GA before moving to their headquarters in Marshfield, WI. I progressed through several positions at the company, finally becoming Recruiting Manager.

My wife had retired before we moved to Wisconsin, and we were both ready for a move back to the sunny South when I accepted a Director of Driver Development position with Southern Cal Transport in Birmingham, AL.

Presently, I own and manage Integrity Driver Placement, LLC, a contract driver recruiting firm. Additionally, I am a "special contributor" to "The Trucker" magazine; the most widely-read trucking publication in the country. That's a fancy way of saying that I write for them part-time. I also write occasionally for the "Bluegrass Today" website, but that's another story. I'm still writing songs, too.

No one can predict the future, and as of this writing, I don't know for sure if I will ever again earn my living behind the wheel of a tractor-trailer. I still have my CDL, and all the endorsements, but these days I'd rather be at home with my sweet wife and the animals, tending the garden and spending my weekends making bluegrass music with friends.

However, I'm proud of the time I spent on the road as I am of all the years I've worked in this wonderful industry. I've met and worked with some great people and seen much that I would have missed if I had never climbed into the cab.

After all is said and done, there's no question:

There's diesel in my bloodline, and highway lines are painted on my soul.

Drive safely. Please.

Cliff Abbott

About the Author

Cliff Abbott has experienced the trucking industry from the backroads to the front office. He has passed his knowledge on to thousands as trainer and instructor. A prolific writer, he has authored safety and training materials, short stories, poems, books. He maintains a songwriting website at www.cliffsongs.com. A truck driver advocate, he still maintains his Commercial Driver's License. He has been published in several magazines and is currently an exclusive, Special Contributor to "The Trucker." He resides in Nectar, Alabama with his wife Thresa, two cats, and a dog.

Cover Art

Michael Cozzi started his career as a professional magician/illusionist and hypnotist performing everywhere from Las Vegas to Atlantic City to an HBO appearance and all points in between. In 1990 Cozzi traded the spotlights for headlights and the open roads of America and for the next 16 years savored the freedoms that only an American trucker can experience and enjoy. He now lives in Alabaster, Alabama with his lovely Bride Danna and their eight pound Maltese, Reilly Sarah Wigglebottom. He owns and manages a video production business, Video Birmingham (www.videobirmingham.com), and works in the safety department for a major transportation company.

What's YOUR story?

Every driver has them; those truckin' memories that bring a smile every time. You could write a book...

But, just in case you *can't* write a book, or you don't *want* to write a book, why not submit your story for the next edition of "Chronicles of an American Trucker?" Author Cliff Abbott will select the best and craft them into book form, changing all the names to protect the innocent *and* the guilty, especially *you*. You'll be credited for the story (unless you wish to remain anonymous), and you'll receive a free autographed copy of the book, along with special discounts if you want to buy five copies for your mother.

Send your stories to:

CHRONICLES OF AN AMERICAN TRUCKER
6344 County Hwy 45
Hayden, AL 35079

Or email them to: ***cliffeabbott@gmail.com***

By voluntarily submitting your story, you freely agree to its use and you also agree not to pursue further compensation. That's important in the event of monster book sales or Hollywood blockbuster movies that the author may luck into.

CPSIA information can be obtained
at www.ICGtesting.com
Printed in the USA
BVHW08s0828230918
528267BV00003B/45/P